Mom Egg Review

2014 Vol. 12

Half-Shell Press
New York

Mom Egg Review is an annual collection of poetry, fiction, creative prose, and art by and about mothers and motherhood. *Mom Egg Review* believes literary work with diverse perspectives of mothers and motherhood belongs in the forefront of contemporary literature and discourse. *MER* promotes and celebrates the creative force of mother artists and nurtures community through publications, media, performances, and workshops.

MER Community—Please join us online!

Website: www.momeggreview.com
Facebook Page: www.facebook.com/themomegg
Facebook Group: www.facebook.com/groups/64824413509/
Tumblr: http://themomegg.tumblr.com
Twitter: @themomegg

Cover Image: "Rosalinda and Pauline" by Eti Wade, Migrant Mothers Series.
Cover Design: Sue Altman www.artworksrockland.com

Mom Egg Review is a member of the Council of Literary Magazines and Presses.

This publication has been made possible, in part, by a grants program of the New York State Council on the Arts, a state arts agency, and the Council of Literary Magazines and Presses. *Mom Egg Review* is grateful for this generous support. *Mom Egg Review* is also grateful for the assistance of The Motherhood Foundation, and for the support of individual donors. With thanks to founding editor Alana Ruben Free and founding publishers, Joy Rose & Mamapalooza.

Mom Egg Review 2014 Vol. 12 ©Half-Shell Press and Marjorie Tesser, 2014. All rights reserved.

ISBN-13: 978-0-9915107-1-9 (Half-Shell Press)
ISBN-10: 0991510712

Mom Egg Review
Half-Shell Press
PO Box 9037
Bardonia, NY 10954

Contact: themomegg@gmail.com

Contents

1.

Deborah Brandon	SHOOK – 2
Amy Lee Heinlen	PANGÆA – 3
Kate Kostelnik	A PREGNANT FICTION WRITER – 4
Genevieve Betts	GENESES – 5
Charlotte Mandel	PERDITA'S MOTHER – 6
Ellen McGrath Smith	THE BABY – 7
Emily Wolahan	HER TINY UNIVERSE BECOMES IMMENSE – 8
Robin Silbergleid	SAGE – 8
Marion Deutsche Cohen	EACH LEARNING – 9
Jamie Asaye FitzGerald	THE NIGHT NURSE – 9
Abigail Templeton-Greene	CRYING IT OUT – 10
Anna Weber	AT THE LITTLE GYM – 11

2.

Ashleigh Lambert	THE TRANSLATOR'S NOTE – 13
Becky Tipper	THE OPPOSITE OF METAPHOR – 14 *nonfiction*
Nicola Waldron	THINGS I TELL MY SON – 15
Cindy Veach	THE EEL – 16
Amy Brunvand	KACHINA – 17
Carolyn Williams-Noren	LOOKING AT AD PARNASSUM – 18
Chelsea Lemon Fetzer	PRODUCTIVITY – 20
Nicole Callihan	NURSING – 21
Margaret Young	FIRST DAY OF TEACHING AFTER MATERNITY LEAVE – 21
Sandra Faulkner	HOW TO POTTY TRAIN WHEN PRESENTING A MANUSCRIPT ON MATERNAL POETRY – 22
Rose Auslander	DEAR WILLA, – 23

3.

Louisa Howerow	MOTHER-CHILD DAY AT THE Y – 25
Shanalee Smith	APPLE KISSES – 26
Elizabeth Johnston	SIGNATURE – 28
Kate Falvey	SHARDS – 29
Andrea Potos	TEENAGE DAUGHTER – 29
Caledonia Kearns	A DAUGHTER'S WORK IS HEARTLESS BY NATURE – 30
Cheryl Boyce-Taylor	LEAVING TRINIDAD – 31
Carol Berg	LASCAUX WOMAN AND DAUGHTER – 32
E.J. Antonio	BE – 33

4.

Samina Najmi	BLIND DATE—35	*nonfiction*
Judy Swann	SOFT—36	
Eve Packer	THE DUKE—36	
Jennifer Martelli	COLOSTRUM—37	
Melisa Cahnmann-Taylor	LESSON IN MODAL VERBS—38	
Rosalie Calabrese	THE QUARRELERS—39	*fiction*
Geeta Tewari	EVACUATION—41	
Seretha D. Williams	HOW DIVORCE WORKS—42	
Lois Marie Harrod	POEM FOR MY DAUGHTER IN A DRY MEADOW—43	
Libby Maxey	FAIR FOOD—44	
Heather Haldeman	IN SEARCH OF MAN—45	*nonfiction*
Cassie Premo Steele	BEGUN IN LOVE—47	
Diane Lockward	NESTING—49	

5.

Andrea Beltran	THE CHILD WE NEVER HAD—50	
Kelly Bargabos	LUCKY ME—51	*nonfiction*
Laura Davies Foley	LIKE SHADOWS—53	
Lisha Adela García	HAUNTED—54	
Lisa A. Sturm	KETTLEBELL HEART—55	*fiction*
Erika Rybczyk	BECKETT—56	*fiction*
Jayne A. Pierce	THE QUEST—57	
Vickie Cimprich	THE APPLE'S BONE: A FOSTER SON—58	*nonfiction*

6.

Kristin Roedell	NIGHT BLUE—64	
Erin Olds	LOST—65	
Matthew Hohner	PSALM 40—66	
Nancy Gerber	LITTLE SCAR—67	*nonfiction*
Mary Jo Balistreri	REMEMBERING WITH A LAST LINE BY NERUDA—68	
Marcia J. Pradzinski	IN THE HOUSE ON EMERSON—69	
Elvis Alves	FOR THE MOTHER WHO IS STILL A MOTHER EVEN THOUGH SHE HAS LOST A CHILD—70	
Jane Frances Harrington	MOVING DAY—71	*nonfiction*
Gabriella Burman	ON FRIDAY NIGHTS—72	*nonfiction*

7.

Melanie Sweeney	EVICTION—74	
Donna Katzin	WOMAN'S WORK—75	
Wendy Vardaman	GENESIS, THE MOVIE—76	
Theta Pavis	THE BLOODBATH—77	
Kristin Procter	BURST—78	*nonfiction*

Emily R. Blumenfeld	IN TRIPTYCH BREATH AND SILK—79
Meredith Trede	JARHEADS—80
Claudia Van Gerven	THE BOY—81

8.

Susan Fox	PIANO RECITAL AT THE OLD FOLKS' HOME—82
John Warner Smith	SONGS WE NEVER HEARD—83
John Minczeski	SHE BECAME—84
Gerard Sarnat	ONCE WE WERE ENEMIES. NOW SHE BELIEVES—85
Issa M. Lewis	MY MOTHER'S HAIR—86
Lesléa Newman	IN THE ICU—87
Kyle Potvin	INSTRUCTIONS TO THE YOUNGEST CHILD—88
Patricia Behrens	APOLOGY TO MY MOTHER—89

9.

Elaine Handley	MATRILINEAL—92	
Claudia D. Hernández	AÑOS DORADOS GOLDEN YEARS—93	
Arlene Weiss	MISS TESSIE—94	*nonfiction*
Elisa A. Garza	WHY STIEGLITZ PHOTOGRAPHED O'KEEFFE'S HANDS—96	
Felice Aull	MY MOTHER'S POWER—96	
Cheryl Boyce-Taylor	THEN ON FRIDAY'S—97	

10.

Pat Falk	HER WORDS—98	
Priscilla Atkins	CANDY STORE—99	
P.A Pashibin	MY MOTHER'S FINGER—99	
Kathryn Kysar	THE BURDEN—100	
Patrice Boyer Claeys	HUNGER—101	
Laura Madeline Wiseman	THE RIGHT SIZE—102	
Jessica Feder-Birnbaum	BUTTERCRUNCH—103	
Jacqueline Doyle	SUMMER FRUITS—104	*nonfiction*
Stephanie Feuer	DRUMSTICK—105	*nonfiction*
Electra Hunzeker	SWEET VALLEY—107	*fiction*
Vicki Iorio	AT 60—108	
Tsaurah Litzky	MY MOTHER TOLD ME—109	

11.

Caroline Beasley-Baker	FAME/RISE-FALL-OF-IT (GERTRUDE STEIN)—112
Christine Swint	NUMBER 1 1948—113
Golda Solomon	IS IT ART OR LAUNDRY ON A CHRISTMAS DAY—114
Elizabeth Lara	SACAGAWEA—116
Zoë Ryder White	IN BROOKLYN—117
Holly Anderson	4 BOVINA POEMS—118

12.

Susie Berg	LOVE IS NO OBJECT—120
January O'Neil	ON THE FIRST DAY OF SCHOOL—121
Martha Silano	SAID THE ENEMY TO THE ENEMY—122
Sadie Ducet	REALLY SEEING THE COFFEE TABLE—123
January O'Neil	WHAT THE BODY KNOWS—125
Lesley Dame	THE ANSWER—125
Fay Chiang	REINVENTION—126
Marjorie Maddox	MY MOTHER'S WEDDING ENDS AT MIDNIGHT—128
Faith Williams	WE ARE ALL EACH OTHERS' MOTHERS—129

IMAGES

Katrinka Moore	Nest—1
Katrinka Moore	Flown—24
Caroline Beasley-Baker	untitled/i don't want no whiskey—34
Eti Wade	Rosalinda and Pauline—61
	Cora and Coleen—62
	Connie and Arvin—63
Hester Jones	"I worked in John Lewis baby department for twenty years."—90
	"I used to knit a lot, socks, we used to have sheep, take wool and knit it."—90
	"I was a telephone operator."—91
	"I used to work in Harrods in the confectionary department."—91
Claudia D. Hernández	In The Distance—111
Ana C.H. Silva	The Organ of Circulation—124

Contributors' Notes—130

Mom Egg Review
2014 Vol. 12

MER 12

Editor in Chief
Marjorie Tesser

Editorial Assistants for MER 12
Cheryl Boyce-Taylor
Jennifer Jean
Tara Masih
Carly Susser
Nancy Vona

Founding Editors
Alana Ruben Free
Joy Rose

EDITOR'S NOTE

Welcome to *Mom Egg Review* Vol. 12!

The paradigm shift of pregnancy and child-raising, mothers' work, mothers' bodies, partnering and going it alone, loss, caring for the ill and dying, nurturing our planet, denouncing injustice, making art-- *MER 12* spotlights work on subject matter often ignored by mainstream media, but pivotal to understanding our human situation. The works are insightful, brave, cynical, tragic and funny. We take great joy in presenting the work of these talented writers and artists, and pride in having published such vital work for a dozen years.

We couldn't do it without you, our wonderful readers and contributors. We value your participation in our community as we keep growing and presenting the best work by and about mothers and motherhood.

Thanks for 12 years, and enjoy the issue.

All the best,

Marjorie Tesser

1.

Katrinka Moore Nest

Deborah Brandon

Shook

it's true i
rose-milk
tea to the shoreline. the
baby set off another alarm the
motherly verb shook.

a very brief stat though it's
a wash it's tacos again &
a door that wouldn't quite

ampersand,

milk teeth tapped the teacup breaking
it dawn is like that the mirror
inside the flower bracing NOW my
callous blooming another
rim raw. tilted

Amy Lee Heinlen

Pangæa

I want this burden
       this swelling belly

             I can't believe   I never did before
                 How silly that girl

      How odd   this woman with a fish in her belly

           I see a picture of a lamb's face
and want to crush its
       cottony ears   black liner lips
           inky marble eyes
      to my swollen stinging breasts
and hug and hug and hug

I want the pastel parties
      with pink-topped roses
          chocolate cupcakes rich as soil
               elaborate packages tiny frilly clothes

A whole world balloons

     My spine is aware
     of how it is a tower
     of tiered pieces

          My sacrum is aware of exactly
              where it tethers
                  to my pelvis   like Pangæa

     the spread   of continental drift   keeps me
        on my side at nights
             slow to straighten
                  from bed to bathroom   slow
                        to lower to the toilet

I am now old and young
     an ancient crater lake
         made fresh from a surprise summer storm

Kate Kostelnik

A Pregnant Fiction Writer

Narratives of characters treated cruelly
would upset my students to a point where
one asked, quite seriously, if we could read
fiction that didn't make him want to "jump off a cliff."
I asked where these Nebraska bluffs were
and lied that I'd gladly assign a cheery story--
if such a thing existed.

Today, I force myself to read my own syllabus.
Flinching at the fictional boy who drinks lye,
or the girl who stays behind to have her skull smashed in
before her assailant "peels down her pink tights and rapes her."
And I wrote that last line. A much younger me who could
kill for the sake of plot and structure.

Today, I close books and look out windows
waiting and worrying it will only get worse--
this heartbreak at having joined the world.

Genevieve Betts

Geneses

1. I thought he would begin
like a low-hanging fruit—
      fleshy and plump
and free of lanugo
dangling from floral shoots.

Ripe, the stem finally snapping—
his avocado body straining branches,
          breaking some
in a tumble along the trunk.

Then the landing—
reaching between aerial roots,
picking him up, brushing off the mud
and touching skin
smelling of earth and wet bark.

2. It happened differently,
more like a hard melon
left in the garden—
      too much time
      to ripen.

Pull and push for days
but it's impossible to pluck it,
the stem too connected
to an offshoot of strong vine.

At last, a gardener with clippers
cuts and clears plant matter,
spawns sliced stems, bruised
leaves, an aroma of sweat—
      picks him for me.

Charlotte Mandel

Perdita's Mother
Photograph, the poet H.D., 1919

Here, I said to the nurses,
I know no rules of mothering.
Blessings upon blank-eyed cows.

Crossing the Aegean
I rode figurehead at the bow.
Your wails for milk
like two clever fists
twisted my breasts.

At Delphi,
instead of a tall thin self
reflected in a rock pool
> *round cheeks*
> *short skirt white blouse*
> *mouth aquiver with, perhaps, laughter?*

At the touch of my finger
endless circles flared from the girl in the water.
Childbirth revises personal myth.

> *Oars do not splash in my dream*
> *Row row row*
> *echoes from glistening cliffs*
> *covered with hieroglyphs..*
> *Tableaux light up as we pass*
> *moon-eyed children supine*
> *on stone floors.*

When I returned
your blue-birth irises shone hazel,
my face a votive
reflected in twin black pupils.
Who was at worship—
you or I?

Ellen McGrath Smith

The Baby

The way the baby grew in me was geodesic; the first Gulf War had come and gone before it was complete. She was portable. We had baskets, slings, so many small containers, each with special handles, and we took her everywhere we went.

The baby was a puzzle to herself and to our faces bending in to see how sounds we made changed the patterns on her face.

The baby's features burnished into her soft flesh; her skin was softer than anything I'd ever touched except water.

Her eyes reflected and accepted what we showed her, she was game for almost anything, except balloons or bubbles blown out from a face.

In her early days, even though we thought she'd just be the cliché lump of clay, she did not roll or sleep or eat in any predictable way.

She slept exactly as she pleased. She started forming words at 5 mos. Those words at first were watercolor. Lines would come much later. Her words blurred with other words we knew, which made us laugh. Ontogeny, phylogeny, the wonder of it all.

In public, as a couple with the baby, we became a couple with a baby, that creature that's so special in one setting, mediocre, even abject, in another where there are a lot of these same creatures filling their expected role, not always well. For instance, shopping malls.

The baby surely knew my thoughts sometimes, even as she rode iconic in my arms, on my hip, as she traveled over years from my calves up to my chin. The baby was exactly what I'd ordered, after all.

Because of where she put me.

Emily Wolahan

Her Tiny Universe Becomes Immense

One cries at this.

Another sleeps through it.

We now have a future of arched
      bridges and cathedral spires.

Now we have each other—

There is no sleep that cannot be interrupted—
her small ear not an inch
from such a small brow.

Robin Silbergleid

Sage

The way the Rabbi hefts the Torah
on Saturday morning, she takes
the child from me, touches her
with winter-chapped hands. No
hesitation at the umbilical stump,
crusty, like a burnt offering. The baby
surrounded by soaps and potions,
I think of sacrificial altars, holy water.

When will my hands stop shaking?
Even Sarah didn't want to let go.

Marion Deutsche Cohen

Each Learning

We show him the inside of the piano, we point and bend, over and under, and at first he points and bends, too, at first he leans forward. But then he must have noticed how crowded it is in there, how dark and how dry, something must have become Proustian, something must have moved the wrong way because he suddenly pulls back, suddenly turns around, suddenly gets that dreamy swollen look, suddenly needs the deepest, the best, the mommy-est part of mommy. He needs his cushion, he needs his register, he needs his safe and his sound. It's time for eating, again and still, time for eating, it so often is.

Jamie Asaye FitzGerald

The Night Nurse

Tenderness burns like an injection
as milk comes down from under arms
into my breasts. Pearly droplets
leap out like tears, a small river flows
over my chest into the bed, the sheets
gathered around her for comfort.

The arrowhead of this love cuts.
When I wake to its exquisite pressure,
she is there for me, her hand fluttering
about my bosom in the dark, her mouth
a salve, ready to take.

Abigail Templeton-Greene

Crying It Out

It is the night we read about,
the night all the moms talk about,
an episode I saw on 'Super Nanny'
and thought *What's the big deal?*

The big deal is it is 4:00 in the morning
and she's been crying since 2:00.
The big deal is with every yowl my boobs ache,
and my heart slaps me in the chest, questioning:
What have I done? What have I done? What are we doing?

She will learn, the doctor says—
her hands gripping the edge of her crib.
Sleep training, they call it—
her small body howling at the monitor,
rocking itself back and forth.

4:23 am: arms flail in desperation,
she reaches to standing,
exhausted, falls back to sitting.

4:50 am: she is up again,
having dragged herself
to the corner of the crib,
cheeks wet with fury,
her plump fingers search in the dark,
hoping for some sign of comfort,
some sign of us.

Every cell in my body wants to pull her
from the pit where dreams don't go,
pull her and wrap her in quilts
that smell like mother, but instead
I stay at my post.

I turn the fan up to high, check the clock,
try not to peak at the screen that shows me

what I don't want to see.
I curl my arms
and feet around my husband
searching desperately
for someone
to mother.

Anna Weber

At The Little Gym

The absurdity of it doesn't escape me:
      a gymnastics class for babies. When
you are very young, we simply sit together

on the giant blue mat. I prop you up
      against my legs like a sack of potatoes,
and at the instructor's command, I stretch

your legs and arms: in and out. Back
      and forth. Up and down. In and out.
Some trippy version of the alphabet song

blares from the stereo, and intermittently,
      a man's voice offers advice: Stretching
is vital for gross motor skill development...

Remember moms and dads: it's impossible
      to love your baby too much... I'm not sure if
I agree with that, but before I can reflect on it,

the class moves on and suddenly
      all of the babies are being lifted up,
hoisted onto our shoulders, paraded

across the room like show-dogs.
      It's too much for one of them, and she
begins to whimper—softly at first.

A quiet complaint. But then it swells
          into a cry, a wail, a tornado siren filling
the room with its red blare. We exchange

looks of pity with each other as the mother
          hauls the baby out. Hey, we've all been there.
Today, I am grateful for your silence.

The man on the stereo is saying something
          about the magic of the inner ear. I place
you back on the blue mat alongside

the other babies. Watch as you all seem
          to drift towards some indecipherable point,
fish endlessly floating with an invisible current.

2.

Ashleigh Lambert

The Translator's Note

The translator stands before you chagrined.
All these obsolete words like *telegram* and *carport*,
cuckoo clock and *wow*
        Tangibles like *semi-colon*
                And *I apologize*; I'm sorry.

Your language is imploding and overcoming itself
and I feel like I should be putting all these sounds around your head.
        I should be using words with umlauts
            or at least saying *umlaut*
since I can't take you to Austria or anywhere useful.
Sheepish, I paste subtitles
        in all your favorite books.

Eventually it'll be *laptop*,
rhinoceros or *stockings*.
Eventually you'll be
        set upon the world
           only I'll be away from you.
They call it planned obsolescence.

My training as a translator is a hill I stand upon.
Your future lies just beyond that grove of trees.
I can't predict the language
        to gather around this fact.
Give me more words to interpret
or at least feed me their phonemes.
        I'll give you the big stool and the small silver spoon.
        I'm only crying so that you'll talk louder.
More of it
        more
                mm mm mm.

Becky Tipper

The Opposite Of Metaphor

The greatest thing by far is to be a master of metaphor. It is the one thing that cannot be learned from others; it is also a sign of genius, since a good metaphor implies an eye for resemblance. - Aristotle.

I keep the things he sloughs off as he races through childhood: the tiny wristband he wore in the hospital, a lock of baby hair. Soon, I will gather up his first lost teeth and wrap them in tissue. It seems the essence of mother-work – collecting these precious discarded things, smoothing them and putting them away.

Along with these things, I keep his words too, catching them before they dissolve into air. I handle them gently, wondering at their beauty. I fold them neatly away to be kept. What delight me most are his metaphors and similes – those moments when the world shifts a little, rearranged by the discovery of sameness in things that once were distinct. They are his first, unwitting, poems.

I note down how once, when he was two, he told me that a small stain was the carpet's bruise. Aged three, newly fascinated by the things his own body could do, he declared, "A cough and a yawn go together like curry and rice." Another time, surprised by a sudden storm before we had time to close the windows, we watched the rain streak in sidelong through the open cracks. "The rain is posting itself in like a letter," he said.

Aristotle wrote that the ability to craft a good metaphor was a sign of genius. Which is not to say that I think my son is a genius (at least no more than any parent who is constantly dazzled at the impossibility of a child), but there is surely something magical in finding similarity where there was none, in connecting the world to itself. And I wonder if when he reads his words years later, having forgotten he ever spoke them, he might recall something crucial and elusive that somehow makes sense of everything.

Aged two, watching the view from the train window as we sped through the English countryside, he told me the electricity pylons straddling the fields were, in fact, "seahorses running by." This summer, as we waited to cross the street and a passing truck puffed out exhaust fumes and hot air, he shuddered and complained, "It coughed on us with its horrible breath." Last week, sitting in the back of the car, he figured out how to control the windows himself. He pushed the button, watched the window slide up slowly and then stopped it halfway. "I drowned half the houses," he announced.

As I watch him sprawled asleep in his underwear this morning – long and lean, all legs and smooth back – he is so unfamiliar and so beautifully strange that I cannot believe he began inside my body, almost indistinguishable from me. And it occurs to me that having a child is itself an act of poetry, a sort of metaphor in reverse. If metaphor is the flash that connects the unconnected, then perhaps its opposite is mothering: not the sudden bringing-together of disparate things, but rather a slow unraveling of what once seemed almost the same.

Nicola Waldron

Things I Tell My Son

Sugar will slow you down,
the spinach make you strong.
A thunder cloud's a mountain upside-down,
its clap a battle, and lightning? That is
electricity.

Yes, Grandma's horse ate maple leaves:
the horse is buried by that tree.
The car got old and had to be replaced.
The little baby died.

Get up or you'll go hungry;
sleep, or you'll be tired.
The moon tonight's a smile: the sun
shines on the moon and makes it bright.

Long ago now, men stood upon that moon,
and jumped.

Cindy Veach

The Eel

He was short, maybe seven inches,
tapered at the tail with yellow
eyes. There were diamonds on his back

like a rattlesnake, but green
as the water he came from.
When my son picked him up, I yelled,

"Put him down. He might be electric.
He might sting." Sunlight
came through his body

and the pattern on his back
variegated into a palette of greens.
The kind of fabric I might

buy without purpose
and save for years.
When I dropped him

back into the water
I watched him swim straight
down. The deeper he went

the darker the weave became
until all I could see
was my own face
looking back at me.

Amy Brunvand

Kachina

The man who made my kachina said,
It's made from cottonwood root
That knows how to reach for water
Deep down under the sand.
He said he paints the eyes on last
Because the spirit enters the wood
When it can see the world for itself.

He said the doll is not sacred;
You give it to your children
So they will get familiar with the sacred
And when they meet the spirit out in the world
They will recognize it.

So I put the kachina up on my wall
Like he told me to
Hoping that I will recognize the spirit
When I meet it out in the world,
Hoping that that my children will learn
How to reach for water
Deep down under the sand.

Carolyn Williams-Noren

Looking at Ad Parnassum

Dear Paul Klee,

I teach my daughters
what diagonal means—*touching
on the corners, but not on the sides.*

In our new game, we lay squares
on a grid—blue, red,
and I bet you've never felt such smoothness
or heard such clatter without glass.

I read that for five years your art
was slow—you had to *divide your time
with domestic matters.*

When I say
soles of my feet together,
do you see me slouch
against the sofa's arm—

half dancer, half boat?
I'm not too old

to be comfortable like this, but my back
pulls taut. I'm built
like your Twittering Machine: The wires
hold me together; the brittle mouths
reach up. I check
to find the tiny things I'm made of.

Are you there, grains of rice? Mouthfuls
of meat? Bites of summer's perfect peach?

How did it feel to slice
the door to the home of poems
heavy as cable thick as my arm
across a thousand tiles?
How did it feel to paint the first rectangle?

Paul Klee, I can still see the circle
when I look away. My bent legs are
those wedges. The zipper of my shirt
touches cool on my cheek. I think you'd like

this zipper's small teeth
and how it sounds—as though something
is ripping—even while it draws two halves together.

Chelsea Lemon Fetzer

Productivity

She knows she is alive she wakes up crack of dawn
                                                          She

stays on top of what needs doing and what needs
doing doesn't run out long as the engine takes oil
and there's a fray on his hem. Mustard weeds and
clover guaranteed to get pulled up before they seed.

She crack of dawn she knows she wakes up is alive
                                                          She

wouldn't believe the bookcase waits in line to fall
apart when it falls in love with her. Sink fakes
broken washer to get her under its cupboard.
The upholstery at last changes her mind on its color.

She is alive she wakes up crack of dawn she knows
                                                       She

says it takes just-so many threads to hold the pants up.
Each a to-do list, follow through to the foot, no
option for unraveling. Does anyone else bother
to put a dish away? Nevermind she'll do it.

she knows she crack of alive she is dawn wakes up
                                                     She

Crouches with warm rag after the vent knits new coat
from dust. Tupperware cabinet out of order in time
for Saturday morning, loyal exhibition, though
her hands are always marked from another's stray nail.

she knows she is alive
                                         She

Won't wait for one more mosquito to trace the wall
before sewing a patch on that screen.

she wakes up crack of dawn
                                         She

Loose tile. Bulb out. Grease stain.

Nicole Callihan

Nursing

Above my desk, I have a photograph
of a woman with two fried eggs for breasts.
They are sunny side-up,
and the woman stares defiantly
into the camera, like, hey, why are you
staring at my chest? She is thin and butch
and beautiful. Me, these days,
fat with burgers and hope and cake,
I keep worrying that Ella
will stop nursing, that I'll go to her,
and she'll turn her head from me,
and that, suddenly, I'll have my body back again.
It will be all mine, and I'll have no idea what to do with it.

Margaret Young

First Day of Teaching after Maternity Leave

Milk vomit on black velvet
looks like a galaxy,

the one we live in,
named for milk.

Sandra Faulkner

How to potty train when presenting a manuscript on maternal poetry

Drink a cold espresso after the coffee line maul.
Catch the conference plane with a wet crotch in your pants.
Think about how you are not a (fill in the blank) mom.

Don't speak of tiny fish crackers, too much
starch and big T-truth makes them antsy,
like a double espresso day line at the mall.

Walk with dry pants to the podium, blink like a mole
fresh from under the school, that darkened land
where we all crawl with bloody knees to this mom

they all want you to be. Now with malice,
No, no   No, do not pant.
Drink that espresso, man.

If you must answer that question about your mind
the biography behind your paper, the argument in the last part
Repeat: "but I am no star mother"

as you curl your fingers by the podium mums
yellowed from the incandescent lights, you can't
ignore the conference attendees' espresso mad,
say, "I don't want to be *your* mommy."

Rose Auslander

Dear Willa,

On this runway to nowhere, the Friday afternoon air is over-salted
with seagulls scolding, "No, no, no," oh my daughter

I want to sleep through this badly-timed business trip
and dream up a way to make it back to Brooklyn

before you give away the last of your old dresses and kisses
and hitchhike into the wild.

My skin already smells like past decades
of airline peanuts, like every trip away,

every trip you'd ask for the little packages of peanuts when I got back.
Now, my eyes won't shut.

The wheels lose touch with the ground. I

                              want to step out of my dark suit

slide over the wings of the plane, past the Hudson River
and wrap myself invisible around you, a shield

                              impermeable as the window

reflecting my hands dimming as I write this letter I know not to send --
as I don't tell you

I hope you are buttering the challah dough I left for you to bake and bring,
I hope you are preheating the oven like I showed you, I

hope you can't hear me whisper,
"Don't burn it."

3.

Katrinka Moore — Flown

Louisa Howerow

Mother-Child Day at the Y

The workshop leader sweeps us into a circle.
I keep glancing away from her dangling seed earings
toward the open door, the children, a room

where my daughter sits drawing. There was a time
she and I were limitless, the sun high on the page.
What I said was once true. A snake eats her own tail,

recreates herself. Release and liberation or was it
circular dependency? Dance shoes discarded,
we measure our inhales, exhales, as if this room

doesn't confine us to being mothers, as if we can
leave aside our children's coughs and stuffed noses.
My daughter slides her bottom across the floor

to sit in the doorway. I exhale audibly, watch
as she pushes her fat red crayon down the paper,
long vigorous lines as if she's digging her way out.

Shanalee Smith

Apple Kisses

I.

Last night, curled on our couch
I was reading Yusef Komunyakaa's
"Boys in dresses"
wholly swallowed by this world
to which I could only ever be witness
I wondered about you
whether you wore your mother's high heels
the way our son does
Did you ever wear dresses?
And at what age, exactly,
did you cease being kissed on the mouth?

I asked, quietly,
this unexpected question
to which you said,
"My mother never kissed me on the mouth"

(I couldn't conceive of such a thing)
You continued,
"I find the way you kiss Oliver creepy"
I bent my head over my book
and pretended to read
You stopped speaking

II.

This morning
Oliver crawled into our bed
after you'd left for work
He curled his body before mine
mimicrying a fetal pose
as if he were still encased by my skin
I pressed my lips into his cheek softly
and kissed him several times
in rapid succession

like the firing of an automatic weapon
It woke me completely
this whisper of your words
I lay with my eyes half open
looking at the reflection
glaring across the bed from me
With my face cradled in the hollow
of his apple-sweet neck
I couldn't get this feeling out of my head.

Elizabeth Johnston

Signature

Your name like I've never seen it—
I curve my finger around
alphabet curling into petals, blossoming at the tips,
tendrils dangling from the S,
a heart languishing over your I.
I am as dazzled now as when first
you rolled to your stomach, rocked to your knees,
crawled across the hardwood to the cat.

When did you learn this?

Once I knew everything about you,
before you were born traced your name in my journal,
in print, in cursive, first name, middle, last,
all your names, all the ways I might write you into being.
But all along, you have been imagining selves I could not,
gathering your weight beneath you,
practicing your reach, pushing off.

Soon I will be begging your secrets--
and you, innocent traitor, will dole them out like cheerios to a baby,
a little at a time to keep me quiet.

Kate Falvey

Shards

You can settle in
pulling scraps of firelight
up over your chin like
a child fighting a flickering dream.

There's no sinking into the dim,
streetlamps blaring salvation
into the empty walkway,
the empty house.

Your child has grown all murky
in the ambient light of coming adulthood.
Those are your shadows on her face, your
lost horizons already thready in her distant eye.

Andrea Potos

Teenage Daughter

I'd been warned
of tempestuous seas
with wakes of long silences,
or rains of moody sleet
pockmarking the house.

Here
now, a squall
comes--but brief--
it leaves
a great shining in its place.

Caledonia Kearns

A Daughter's Work is Heartless by Nature

Hands down being the daughter
is better, putting on the blue sweater,
kissing your single mother at the door
as nipples strain against cashmere, insides
thrum with the anticipation of exposure,
how steam will cover everything
when hot and cold refuse to part.
The mother requires finesse—
a stretch-marked Venus on the half-shell
minding the store. A daughter's work
is heartless by nature though hard to admit.
You might think you love me more,
can't yet see you will cross oceans,
board planes, run fast, then faster
while my heart bleeds. But loss
can be learned. It just takes practice.
Don't look back. Eat the six seeds.

Cheryl Boyce-Taylor

Leaving Trinidad

I stumbled down the stairs
of the Port-of-Spain general hospital
into the broad yellow light
morning with her band of sorrow filling my heart

I wanted to take the stairs back up three at a time
grab my mother out of her sick bed and beg
don't let me leave you mammy
don't make me go   please let me stay

praise Uncle Alvin with his warm arm
and small voice
be a good girl Sherry, he said hugging me close
do your school work   listen to Aunt Ena
America will be your new home   that's not so bad

your mammy will join you in a few months
I promise to help her get well
I'm counting on you
yuh not a pretty girl   but yuh smart
yuh brain big and yuh mouth bigger   make old Uncle proud

I barely heard anything Uncle Alvin said
my body swelled with sobs
in one hand my traveling bag
in the other an oversized brown envelope with my chest x-ray's

I would have to present the x-ray to customs to gain entry into the U.S.
the x-ray would prove that I did not have tuberculosis.

Carol Berg

Lascaux Woman and Daughter

her open mouth of hunger
    small sparrow with dangerous wings
  plaiting her hair soothing my fingers

the pigs in the muck surprise us with their gnarled noise of panic and routing
    all nose in roots and mud

the green dragonflies bring the sheen of water on their wings
  I wish for water's reason

how to bring her to the paths of dead deer how to show her to stay clear
    when she sees the burning awaken in the eyes of men to dance around
        the snapping jaws of men

oh when can we dance around the circular table

somewhere in the air it smells of rain

    her hair moving like the rain

the delicate rain running inside her

E.J. Antonio

Be
(A poem for my daughter, Jessica)

be chipped wine goblet, bent soda can, crushed water bottle, cracked cup tea bag dipped in hot sauce, be Passover grape juice spilled in crack of sidewalk. life bends you lets you fall cause it can. stand up. when you be piss pot full a life's crap be rain. wash it all away. be blessing in flame, amen in prayer, be every stone skipped 'cross lakes and rolled from tombs. say grace, remember who was in the sky when you were born. be whistle if you can. hum if you can't. clouds want to hear your song. be tears in Mingus ballads. the sun wants to bake you 'til you is sweet crunch of slab bacon rind, burn you black-eye peas stuck-to-the-pot-bottom strong. let it. those little bits of hard got your grand-mommas over when the soul looked back and cried. be water dancin' on hot skillets flauntin' belly rolls, hips, dropped bosoms, wrinkles, gray hair where you figured it would be and everywhere you never imagined. too many can't flaunt it, and a whole lot won't get the time to signify about it. be canyon echo, whisper in dogwood blooms, wind in hawk feathers. be that wish you dreamed walkin' long Harlem avenues, Mount Vernon parkways, Bronx roads, Yonkers highways Philadelphia streets… and when you stop say…

i was Lilith, Lazarus, woman at the well, was part god, part devil and a whole lot of breakdown stuck in a Son House whine. a whole lot of conflict wrapped in a Frieda Kahlo stare.

but i was damn happy

4.

Caroline Beasley-Baker — untitled/i don't want no whiskey

Samina Najmi

Blind Date

At twenty-one, my mother has striking eyebrows—expansive, dark, and gently converging. Lush like Lalmonirhat's hills that cradle the white colonial building she calls home. My father sees her for the first time during the wedding ceremony, reflected in a mirror. His heart beats easier at the sight of her light-skinned face, her downcast eyes, and still lips, which have never been painted before this night. But the fine hair that rims those lips, and especially those eyebrows, so bold, so black, and sharply angled make him unsure of his ability to keep her. Throughout their 23-year-old marriage, my father will have a recurring nightmare in which another man carries his wife away. (Until one does.) His howls will awaken the sleeping children.

A good Pakistani bride of the sixties, my mother doesn't open her eyes to look upon her groom's face until the throng of *geet*–singing women in brilliantly hued, silk saris have ushered her to the bridal chamber. They sit her down on a bed strewn with roses and gardenia, scooping the emerald silk of her flamboyantly flared *pajama* after her. A paisley print of solid silver splashes across both the *pajama* and red tunic in provincial Bihari fashion—much to the bride's dismay, who had hoped for something trendier from the stores of the big city where, she hears, the groom and his sister live together. The singing women help her cross her left leg and bend the right one, resting her chin upon her knee. They place her hennaed hands in a clasp around the knee--artfully, so that the bejeweled fingers of her right hand cover the shriveled left one that doesn't open. Adjusting her vermilion-and-gold *dupatta* over her head one last time, they exit, still singing of maiden temptresses and the fast-beating hearts of their suitors, satisfied to have staged just the right degree of bridal modesty and mystery.

When the groom and bride are finally alone, he lifts her veil of garlands as gently as he can. A *teeka* with a single ruby at its center glimmers on her forehead, its tiny white pearls brushing against those startling eyebrows. A fine hoop of gold, the bridal nose-ring she will never wear again. The groom's shapely hand reaches for her chin and tips it up from the knee, ever so slightly. As if on cue, the bride opens her eyes. She sees the slim, dark man her parents have chosen for her, an assistant professor of physics in faraway Karachi. Her eyes take in the crisp white shervani collar that encircles his neck, the wedding turban he will never wear again. The severe, pencil-thin moustache that restrains the generosity of his full lips. She looks into his big, dark eyes and wonders at their melancholy. And what she feels for him is not the heady passion of the romances she has secretly been writing.

The man seems kind, if remote, as virginal as she is, and they spend the night telling the stories on which their forevers will depend. At twenty-nine, he already feels his life ebbing. The bride doesn't know yet how greedily death claimed his young parents.

In the bathroom she prays for love to grow in her heart.

Judy Swann

Soft

The ferns, those old souls, babbled with the nightjars
and I with the man who loved to smile.

"The ferns are blooming," I said.
"Ferns never flower, he said, for they are cryptograms."
"Sounds like military work," said I.

"This is the time of year they bloom."
Later said my smiling man, "When the nightjar flies,
kids sleep at the mother's breast."

For many years I did not want to bring a man
home, where my linen smells of the line,
where I close the west windows at night.

"Oh," he said, "you are so soft."

Eve Packer

the duke
after sappho

deduke men a selanna
kai Pleiades mesai de
nuktes para d'erkhet ora
ego de mona katheudo

moon down in lovers
arms dovestars kiss/coo-
ing under wave, bed, me
alone mid-night/night/-
time
        goes by

Jennifer Martelli

Colostrum

The dinosaurs in the movie are cloned female,
certain hormones suppressed, and yet

some mutate into males,
and they breed. They are hungry

all the time. I've never been
so large as now. I make cleavage

watching TV next to my husband,
mindlessly touch and press

my own breasts beneath his faded
red chamois shirt.

The drop of clear pre-milk
satisfies no one's ache. It is

tasteless. He licks the tip of my finger,
You're a mammal, he says,

and almost looks relieved.

Melisa Cahnmann-Taylor

Lesson in Modal Verbs

I can use a phone, meaning that I am able to,
I have the ability to dial, to speak, to listen,

to be brief or extended as required
by economy and opportunity. This is a skill

unlisted on any resume but unmitigated, hedgeless,
like I can pick up the kids, put milk on a third shelf,

Swiffer wood floors, fold t-shirts by exact specifications.
In the South one *might could* remember Mothers' Day

before Mothers' Day and one *might could* shave
in a way that doesn't leave evidence of one's entire manly self

like a drought's ant invasion, or one *might could* tell the other
one has taken care of dinner, baby sitters, gifts for one's

mother. One uses *can* to talk about the present or future, abilities
achieved, such as one *can* breathe, one can take our daughter

to the bathroom before bedtime, one *can* run but one *can't* hide
from hypothetical pasts for which we employ could

as in I *could have* danced all night had you asked me which you *could have*
but didn't. Can I ask you a question?

You for whom English is second nature, you who should know better,
who *could have* asked for clarification, directions, who *would have*

if you had been me? Would you like to take lessons
in our language? Between pick up and drop off,

after snackbowls and bedtime stories, we can start
by studying requests and politeness conventions, move

to adverbs of manner followed by wishes and infinitives,
the verb phrase, *to be*, as in *happily ever after*.

Rosalie Calabrese

The Quarrelers

"Aaaiiieee!" A woman's scream derailed my own tortured sleeplessness. David, wrapped like a pig-in-a-blanket, rolled over and groaned. A layer of satin-covered fiber-fill muffled his voice.

"What's that?"

"A scream," I said, although officially I wasn't speaking to him following our latest fight. "Oh." He burrowed deeper under the quilt.

"Aiee . . . help . . . stop . . . don't . . . ." A string of pleas penetrated the bedroom walls. Then a thud. I bolted upright.

"Nobody's business," David mumbled. "Sleep."

Miraculously, the noise stopped. I lay down, careful not to let our bodies touch in case he got the idea that I forgave him, and returned to agonizing over our growing inability to agree on any subject — even a vacation: he wanted to go skiing; I had visions of long walks on a sunny beach. But I knew that wasn't what really bothered me.

We had never argued about anything before I had talked about getting pregnant. David said it would interfere with his career track. I told him he was being silly. He told me I could look for another husband. Now I was beginning to think I should. No way would I allow us to end up like my parents who had hardly spoken to each other for the past twenty years. I felt myself nodding off, thoroughly depressed. Suddenly the ruckus started again, louder than before.

"Help . . . help." The sobbing voice pounded on me; I pounded on David.

"Wake up," I insisted. "I think she's being murdered. We have to do something."

"Like what?"

"Call the police."

"Oh, Christ. We'll be up all night," David said.. He got out of bed and flicked on a light.

The woman's cries were incessant now. I picked up the phone and dialed 911. I could hardly hear the questions being asked, but finally the message got through.

"Five minutes," I reported to David.

Hearing people gathered in the corridor, we put on the robes we had given each other for Christmas and went out to join them. After five of the longest minutes on record, two uniformed men stepped off the elevator. We pointed them in the direction of the disturbance. They took the stairs two at a time. Banging and yelling was soon replaced by a spooky hush. I stood next to David and hugged myself until the policemen reappeared.

"It's okay, folks. You can go back to bed," they announced.

Our band of self-appointed guardians, though exhausted, was disgruntled.

"What'ya mean? What's going on up there?"

"Just a family quarrel. Forget it. . . . Go home and get some sleep."

Did David write their script, I wondered, or do all men think alike?

The next morning, while David was taking a shower, I heard something scrape against the apartment door. I went out and found a note written in black Magic Marker. "YOU EVER CALL COPS ON US AGAIN YOU DEAD."

"Daaaviiid . . . ." I wailed as I ran toward the bathroom and hollered at him to shut the water off. Shaking, I read him the note while he dried himself. "I think they mean it," I said.

David remained silent.

"I really thought he was going to kill her. That's why I called the police."

"I know."

"You're not angry?"

"No. You?"

"No."

He shuffled toward me like a shy kid offering to share a lollipop with a new friend.

"Listen . . ." I said, fingering the hairs on his chest as if they were worry beads. . . . "I've been thinking about Mount Snow and that cute cabin we rented the last time we were there."

"Oh? Well, maybe next year." He let the towel drop as he slid his arms around me. "I've decided Hawaii's not such a bad idea after all."

Geeta Tewari

Evacuation

I cut my hair yesterday,
And my husband did not notice

The six inches of black
Missing from my head,
Sitting dead and quiet in the wicker basket
I chose to make a garbage can.

Today I took my hair to the garbage chute,
And watched it fall into the metal mouth
To darkness, to dirt,

And I felt so relieved.

Seretha D. Williams

How Divorce Works
After "White Couch" by Cornelius Eady

That the court ordered
him to pay
ten years ago,
before the twins were born,

when the toddler was one
and she returned to work
grading essays
in between expressing milk is not enough.

This is how divorce
works: he leaves and
lives a different life; she
stays with babies and bills.

The house settled for
to accommodate his means-
ranch-style, three bedrooms,
no garage- seems small.

This is how divorce
goes: she does her chores
and his; he makes
excuses about why he cannot see the kids;

neither is happy; each sees
the other as better off.

Lois Marie Harrod

Poem for My Daughter in a Dry Meadow

The wild carrots in this field
float, small and spindly on their stalks.

If I could give them iron spindles
I would, such delicate compositions,

star within star in their baskets
which dry into birdcages

of dried flowers, as if someone's
wedding bouquet turned inward

and withered. As it is happening
to you, so unexpected, others yes,

but not this man, you stagger
disbelieving through the grass.

Where is the May that does not wither
into August. What can I say?

Everything seems as bleak
as the cicadas drumming

their numb roil. Talk of the life
you still carry in you–

no comfort. How could Ceres
imagine planting seeds again.

Oh, my daughter, my darling flower,
you have become war or worse.

Abandoned, alone, walking slowly
where once you ran.

Libby Maxey

Fair Food

The children said they saw you as we stood
In line. I heard you then, explaining, calm,
Your measured conversation plain and good
Like cooling bread, an apple on your palm
Outstretched, a table set for autumn with
A cloth and cotton napkins on the left.
Such clean, inviting words—no bitter pith,
No blemished shell, no disconcerting heft.
Our scalding, fried indulgence now in hand,
I turned and watched you as we found a place
To perch and share one plate three ways. Behind
The crowd you moved away in silence bland
And insufficient, hunger in your face,
Your downward glance like biting at the rind.

Heather Haldeman

In Search of Man

    Over cereal this morning, a text pops up on my iPhone.
    Moving ahead with the divorce and needing to practice dating skills. I think I've been on four dates in my life and need to practice, practice, practice.
    It's my work friend, Beverly.
    Therapist says I need to either start online dating or ask friends to set me up. Hate the idea of online. Know any eligible bachelors?
    Since I've been married 34 years, none come immediately to mind. Yet, who better to give Beverly advice than my eighty-six year-old mother who found 3 husbands. She's a widow now. Still wears false eyelashes. And, still considers herself a "pro" at finding eligible men.
    I text Beverly back. *I'm working on it.* Then, tap "Mom" on my contact list. Her number comes to life on the smartphone screen.
    My mother is slowing down, or as she puts it: "the wheels are coming off." But when it comes to her favorite subject – men – she's as sharp as a tack. With my mother, it's always been about a man.
    After our usual morning greeting, I tell her about Beverly.
    "So, what do you think about online dating, Mom?"
    "It's iffy. Never know. And, everyone is like - 12."
    "Actually, Mom, there are dating sites for older people."
    "Still, it's a pig-in-a-poke. She'll have to kiss a lot of frogs before she finds a prince."
    "But, some people have luck…"
    "Not my thing," Mom says, cutting me off. "Listen, pay attention. Tell her these are sure-fire ways…
    Hang with people who are square. Not jazzy.
    Go to any bookstore – they have them still, right? Drop your handkerchief in the Travel section.
    Learn about sports. Any sport. That's what men like.
    Go to anything and everything. Tell her no man is going to come knocking at her door while she's watching TV.
    Never turn down any invitation – especially church.
    Go everywhere even if it's to the 'Daughters-of-I will Arise.' Go. You never know who you'll meet."
    This one makes me laugh. They all make me laugh. "Who thinks this way, Mom?"
    "I'm not finished. Are you writing this down?"
    "Sorry, Mom. Go on."
    Go the market between 6:30 and 8:30pm. Men shop then.

Find another single female friend who belongs to a private club. Get her to take you as her guest – offer to pay the guest fee. Worth it. Keep your eyes open for the single men there.

Never go outside without your face on.

Nails and hair done, too."

"Mom, this all sounds like some sort of old-fashioned fem-fatal advice column."

"Men don't change. They still want the same things. Trust me."

"Finding a man after a divorce," I say. "It's a lot of work."

"Damn right," Mom says. "Keeping one is, too. Now, tell her once she starts dating a man, here are some rules…

Find out if they like their mother. Very important. 9 times out of 10, that's how they'll treat you - eventually.

Find out their horoscope. Earth. Fire. Water…Air - make sure you're a match. That your water doesn't put out his fire.

Be laugh-y. Men want to be amused.

Don't ever mention money. If you say you're poor. They'll run. If you say You're rich, well, that isn't good, either. You might get stepped on, and they might take all your money.

Always, ask about their day. They'll ask you about yours, but they're really only interested in theirs."

"Mom, that's not true."

"You asked my advice. You think it's not still a man's world?"

"If all else fails," she sighs, "tell her to go to Alaska. It's cold as hell, but it's the place to go for men. There's a much better ratio of men to women.

"That's it?" I say.

"That's it."

"Thanks, Mom, I'll pass along your thoughts as soon as Beverly gets back from her camping trip."

"Wait! Camping? Does Beverly hike?"

"She climbed Mt. Whitney two years ago."

"Oh, that's a real plus. She might find a European doing that. European men: they like hiking and all that crap."

"Bye, Mom," I laugh. "Talk to you later."

I tap "End" and begin a text to Beverly:

I pause, thinking back to the couple in their 50s I'd met last week at a business dinner. They'd met online. They are now going on a two-year relationship. "Happy as clams at high tide," the woman had said, adding: "It's an equal relationship. Give-and-take."

I want this for Beverly. She needs to meet and match. Not hook and reel in.

I tap, *Join Match.com*. Still, my mother's voice reigns in my head. Before I press "Send," I add, *Call me when you get back from camping. Lot's of Mom's ideas to share. In the meantime, look out for European men on the hiking trail. Mom says that they love to hike.*

Cassie Premo Steele

Begun in Love

May night dark breeze
       flies through the screen
             candle glows
                   tea cold
                          blanket from Germany
                              wrapped
                                  around my thighs.

And I am not this.
                       Or that.

Just as this is not exactly night
                 but the final rest
                       before the morning
                           dawns
                        a day

that will end with my daughter and
               mother and
                     woman lover
                 with me

on the land where the trees and creek
        have sheltered me.
                I have called this home.

It is not this.
                       Or that.

It is the green turning earth
      that swells
            with the tides
                 of our birth
          and
              connects
     to the blood in me,
            the sea

        of what I am worth.

This round world.
        This body.
              This mother-daughter
                    journey.

Begun in love, resting through
        the night in love like grasses
            that cry dew drops
                until the morning
                    and let birds drink
                        from their tears.

All love is wet and small and giving
        like this.

It is this.
                      And that.

Diane Lockward

Nesting

Outside our window, a robin perched
in last year's nest, a scraggly bundle

tightly tucked behind the light fixture
and dangling sticks and strings.

You came to look, both of us surprised
to see a robin in an abandoned nest—

like a vagrant in a condemned building.
When she flew out, we saw a new nest

inside the old, last year's broken shells
buried under the new abode, bracing it

like a foundation of crushed stone,
and I thought how it has been like that

for us, building a new life inside the old,
how we have woven something new

out of fragments,
what we'd thought ruined, somehow

salvaged, the ghost of the old nest
always shadowing the new one,

as next to me, a man with silver hair,
while on the other side of the glass,

the girl I once was, the boy I once knew,
their faces still unbroken,

behind them, the apparition of a child,
his eyes sun-lit, his hair thick and dark.

5.

Andrea Beltran

The Child We Never Had

At a restaurant nowhere near
the city we both live, I notice
you don't recognize me—
I choose to remain a stranger.

You sit, fixing your cup
of tea, reminding me of how
I'd find you waiting for me
those mornings we'd leave our spouses

sleeping while we snuck in breakfasts
at dawn. Tonight, as a little girl nudges
ribbons of amber curls into your side,
you lean in, your face touching hers,

and call her Mia, the name we had agreed on
years ago. And she is yours,
but not mine. I remember standing behind you
watching you fix your tea,

your long fingers stirring
honey into the cup, amber eyes
fixed on the one small moment
of creation and completion.

Kelly Bargabos

Lucky Me

"You're lucky" my hairdresser says while folding another square of aluminum foil around my freshly painted strands. "No, not lucky, smart. That's it. You're smart." It takes me a second to catch up with her; I had zoned out while she recited the details of her impending night—picking her three kids up from the babysitter, macaroni & cheese and hot dogs, baths and bedtime.

"Must be nice to have all that free time" is what I usually hear from people. I don't tell them about the meals I serve at the soup kitchen, or the children I taught at my church for seventeen years, or that I take my niece school shopping every fall and go to her teacher conferences because her parents can't or won't or how I take my brother to his doctor's appointments and pay his bills. I don't tell them I have less free time than most people I know.

"Do you have children?" has always been a conversation killer, especially when I offer no explanation or answer beyond, "No, I don't." I don't tell them my husband has two from a previous marriage. They have a mother that was there when they were born, when they took their first steps, when they got on the bus for the first time and when they were in trouble. Sure, I tagged along to baseball games, fought with them over dirty socks and tried to convince them to eat my cooking, but none of that ever felt title-worthy. And so I don't say anything.

It was my mother who said "If I had to do it all over again I wouldn't have kids." I don't remember how old I was the first time I heard it and she doesn't remember saying it. But she did and it was okay. It was said without malice. I didn't tell her that when I played with my dolls I never imagined how many I would have or what their names would be. I knew my mother loved me. And I knew she wanted to leave. I knew when my sister and I stood at our front door with the icy air blowing up our flannel nightgowns. She was in the car in the driveway with my father at her window. We screamed and cried and begged her not to leave. She didn't. I knew she had nowhere to go and no money to get there.

I was so secure in my non-motherhood that I married someone who didn't want any more than the two he already had and then convinced him to have a vasectomy. It was his mother who said "a vasectomy is a license to cheat." I smiled and said nothing, relieved I would never be trapped with five kids and no money when he betrayed me.

When I was twenty-two my cousin's wife said "Look how cute you are – all three of you with your little tummies" as my pregnant sisters and I walked in the family reunion. I smiled and said nothing as my face turned a shade of red that clashed with the fluorescent orange jumpsuit I wore. I didn't tell her that I wasn't pregnant and that my paunchy tummy was simply the result of eating too much and weak stomach muscles. My sisters were kind enough to blame it on the jumpsuit. I watched their bodies grow and change while they compared sonogram pictures and water retention levels. Their bodies were never the same after giving birth. I've yet to come up with something that will explain my stretch marks, weak bladder and sagging breasts.

I witnessed my nieces and nephews grow up with familiar faces and habits. I felt like I was watching my brothers and sisters grow up all over again, only this time I wasn't with them, I was watching them. And when my twenty-one year old niece sat with me on the couch and said "I have news. I'm pregnant." I cried. I cried all through dinner, when I got home that night, and the next day. I didn't tell her that now I knew for sure my time had passed. There will be no one on this earth who has my eyes, or my laugh or my voice. There's no better version of me on the way. I didn't tell her that I thought it would be enough to be the cool aunt who always had gum, sleepovers and extraordinary Christmas presents.

So now, tonight, with my head full of aluminum foil and hair dye dripping down my forehead, I nod at my hairdresser in the mirror and give her the smile. I don't tell her I don't feel lucky. Or smart. I'm pretty sure she doesn't mean it anyway, but mostly I wish she would just stop talking.

Laura Davies Foley

Like Shadows

I call my youngest child,
institutionalized for six years, home.

I call her home to sleep
in a room her own again,

no return to "school" possible.

I spend two hours alone,
before she wakes,

two hours of quiet
at my kitchen table,

not enough hours, looking out
at the autumn fog

as birds like shadows
pass by mine.

Lisha Adela García

Haunted

A false disguise for a daughter
whose brain chemicals ran amok
and ruined me,
the mother in me,
the human,
and replaced it with a holocaust
of muscle memory.

Since,
I am a flute
a hollow reed with holes for notes
not bothering the wind
for sound or movement.

The body works,
mind, arms and torso walk—
sustain the outer husk,
but the music of the desert stars
fades into a rattler's
nest in acequia rocks.

I try the hummingbird prayers,
its ruby throat and rapid green darting
hook my breath
bait enough beauty to hear a small aria
in the curl of a leaf,
and maybe, for just a moment,
the sun will lend its light to my bark.

Lisa A. Sturm

Kettlebell Heart

The woman stands across from me in the crowded theater lobby asking about my children, whom she hasn't seen in several years. I know what she is expecting; a list of their latest activities, their proud accomplishments, an accounting of what all the hard work, both theirs and mine, has produced. She has already recited her own laundry list of laudable achievements. Were they lies? No, of course not, her kids just happen to be successful. Some people are lucky that way.

I have two children about whom I can easily speak. "Yes, my oldest is doing well, he finished college last year. Fortunately he found a good job and has a small apartment in the Village that he's sharing with his best friend from high school. I just love his girlfriend and hope they'll get married in a few years. My daughter is a honey; Tennis team, piano, very studious, even loves to bake! Somehow she doesn't hate us yet – amazing for a teenager, don't you think?"

I hope that the conversation will end here. Aren't they opening the theater doors? But no, the well intentioned woman has a good memory and asks about my other son, the son who makes my heart feel as big and heavy as a kettlebell.

Something is catching in my throat. What should I share with her? Should I tell her that I've spent days searching the supermarkets for a certain kind of chocolate and mint filled pretzel that he likes, so that when I visit him at the psychiatric unit of the local hospital, he will smile and have a moment of happiness? Should I tell her about the wave of nausea that often passes over me as I approach my home, fearing that this time he's been released too soon, fearing that all my efforts to save him will have failed, fearing the worst?

Maybe I should tell her the truth; that I don't care whether or not he finishes college or finds a job, that all I want is for him to wake up every morning and take air into his lungs and continue to walk upon the planet. Perhaps I should tell her about the prayers that flow from my mother's parched lips and my own bitter heart, or even the dark moments when I scream at God, my chest a tangled nest of anguish as I beseech heaven to, "save my son!"

And if I did tell her the truth; if I told her that he is a handsome, intelligent, loving, incredibly creative and talented young man who despite years of undergoing every psychiatric treatment under the sun, still may soon take his own life – if I told her all of that, what would she say? What could she say? Would she even want to know?

"He's a sophomore at Rutgers," my eyes smile in her direction. "Enjoy the show."

Erika Rybczyk

Beckett

I watch as my mother purses her lips tightly and shakes her head.

"I told your father not to bring you kids out there. It was an accident waiting to happen; but he dragged you out there anyhow, sure I was being ridiculous."

My mother's gnarled hands impatiently sweep away the crumbs from this mornings toast left on the faded gold specked Formica.

"I pulled that old green arm chair up to the window and pretended to read so that I could see you three. I knew it wouldn't be long before there would be some sort of accident.

Beckett was just toddling, so that couldn't have made you more then 8. It was beautiful on the lake that day."

Her eyes look through the smeared glass over the sink, and she smiles. I know she isn't seeing the rusted swing set, or the dry dead grass, but light dancing on water so blue it seemed black.

"Of course the thing about the cabin - and I'm sure you remember this - was the handful of slippery rocks out back. From there it was right into the water some 6 feet deep.

Ten minutes in and there's the two of you on your knees peering into the water, loaded down with sticks and buckets and SPLASH! , in goes Beckett."

She throws her arms up with a long swoop, then smacks them on the table as she drops into her chair. I guess it's her way of indicating the impact his tiny body made as it hit the water, and then the way it sunk like a stone.

"Your father jumped in and fished him out. He was soaked to the skin, screaming and crying. You and your father were as white as ghosts."

Her fingers slowly trail the seam of the scarred wooden table where she has eaten almost every meal of her last 70 years. She licks at her finger and wipes at an old stain.

"Of course everything was fine, you two were out on the rocks later that same afternoon with your father hovering like a hawk."

My mother stands slowly and reaches for the dogs leash as she heads for the door. She leans her frail body down to gently ease the collar over Lady's head.

"Of course if we knew than what we knew later, we would have let him drown."

Jayne A. Pierce

The Quest

Raw and bleeding
the keyboard cuts fingers
digging into hidden holes
in the privacy settings
for anything on my daughter.

I have enlisted an army:
her youngest cousin
college professors, librarians, teachers
recent high school graduates
my one tech savvy sister
I am famished.

Like using Chines fishing nets
found in Cochin, India
stumping archaeologists in the 1800s
my skills are rusty
tarnished by desperation
expired immunizations
my quest, a mother's disease.

Security compromised
new portrait pic on Facebook
black and white
smiling, her teeth straightened
June pearls hanging from her ears
around her tiny neck
hint of makeup
shoulders barely naked
touched by a swath of dark material
her straight light brown hair
junior prom?

Vickie Cimprich

The Apple's Bone: A Foster Son

March 25, 1991 Five, bright and lively, 35 pounds, bruised and scared green shitless. He was being tied into bed each night. 11 p.m.: still sitting on the floor of his room, Superman pajamas soiled. "Oh, you must feel really bad," I said and gave him a lick of Pepto Bismol. In wonderment he exclaimed, "That's what's wrong with me. I'm sick."

Easter Running after his bigger, stronger foster cousin: *I'll beat you, you cocksucker*. Saturday morning I could see he was cold, sitting in front of the TV cartoons. When I draped the afghan over his shoulders, he asked if I was tying him up.

April Dr. Burns's diagnosis of malnutrition cinches his career in foster care. The newspaper details his stepfather's behavior. The prosecutor, assistant commonwealth attorney, says he was rolled in a sheet "like a mummy" and forced to stand for as long as eight hours. Also forced to eat hot sauce and given ice cold baths.
John and Vickie have become a new couple: Don and Mickey. Treatment for otitis media and speech therapy will sort us all out. The adults are exhausted. Poop on the carpet, on John's shoe, on the toilet seat and down the kid's legs.

His favorite things: books ("Big Gary don't got no books at his house"), clay, blowing bubbles, Leggoes. He has seven stars on his calendar for seven consecutive days of clean, dry sheets. Responds well to corny tricks like "Boy, I'm sure glad you're not eating any green beans because if you do you might grow."

As I cored an apple, he asked if I was taking out the bone.

May 13 Mother's Day. He gives me handfuls of wild strawberries from our back yard.

June 8 One night he prays his heart out, longing to be back with his mom. I'd been singing a Celtic lullaby with its alleluias. He sings:

>
> Wuwa wuwa
> Gah-od
> why did you do-oo that?
> Oh Gah-od,
> whatever you say,
> we will do-oo it.

Sept. 30 Wouldn't get out of bed this morning. When I said the consequence would be not getting to wear his Batman sweatshirt, he got dressed except for his shoes. Came down and spit in John's face. I got a fingernail scratch on the forearm trying to hold him for chair time.

October 18 This morning he waved his socks in the air and announced "These are the socks of evil!" Five years old and laughing at stock -- or sock!-- cartoon cosmologies.

November 1 His aunt's custody petition hearing today. If he's still going to be here for his birthday, I'll send out the Ninja Turtle invitations from the party pack I got at Children's Palace.

I'm so disturbed that after lunch I secretly fish chocolate out of his vast Halloween stash and eat it.

November 14 Big day. Visit with Mom. ("When can I go back to live with her?" "I don't know" etc. etc. He said sadly, "I know. I can't because he hurt me too bad." Last week she asked him to bake cookies for her, so we did and he was proud.

One day we met her while shopping in town. I held out my hand. She hugged me saying "A handshake isn't good enough for the one who's taking such good care of my son."

Nov. 27 "Six years old! Did you ever think you'd make it?"
          "No -- some days when I was at my old house I thought I'd be dead."

June 4, 1992 "Do cows know that they're cows? Then what do they think they are?"

June 22 After goodnights, he says he loves his first family and mom more than John and me. I say I understand and that they're lucky to have him.

March 14 Enraged, he grabs our small marble cricket box and shatters it on the hardwood floor. "Karate-"kicks at me a few times, the pleasure of a new achievement on his face.

January 15, 1993 Tuesday he threw a big one at after-school program: biting, walking on tables, refusing time out. Three days' probation. I tell him that ADHD kids have the same consequences for behaviors as all kids.

August 21 On and off he mouths at me. For a while I can hold out being a safe, solid person he can be mad at for all the turmoil in his life. Earlier this morning he gave me a big hug.

December 1 Reminiscing: His birth mom made the best tasting pork chops. If only he could get enough or any. (It's emblematic: her mother love would be the best, but there's never been enough of it for him.)

January 18, 1994 With fighting -- Ninja Turtles, Power Rangers, other kids and adults -- it's plosives and sibilants. But now and again contentment settles in and he sings

>   Lapidi doo
>   Lapidi dee

Eti Wade   Rosalinda and Pauline

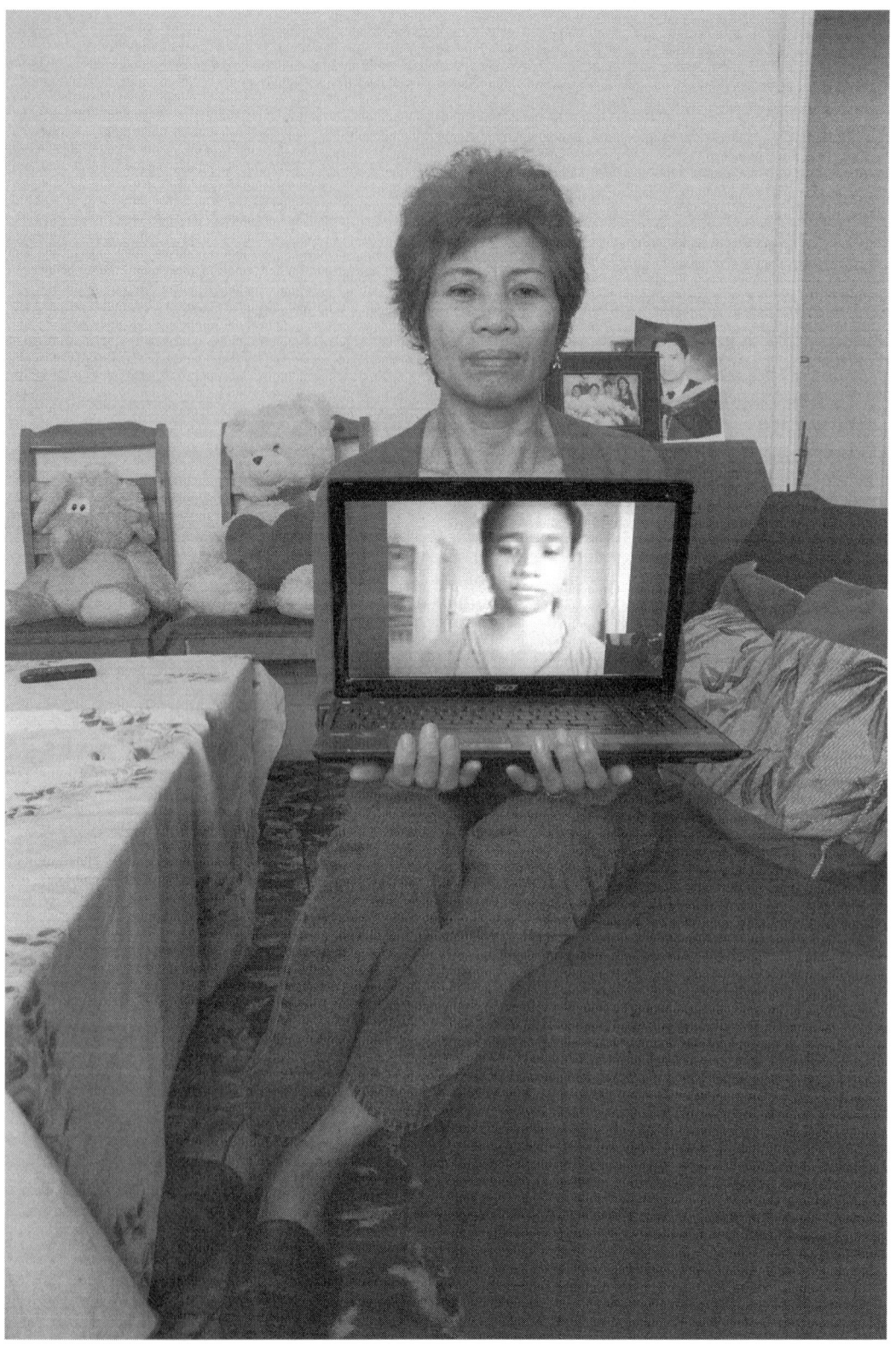

Eti Wade   Cora and Coleen

Eti Wade   Connie and Arvin

6.

Kristin Roedell

Night Blue

Blood in the bath slips
away from a woman
whose monthly seeping
is bound to the moon
with a crimson ribbon.

Her child, astray,
is a pause, a pearl,
a drop of rain.
Wings whirring,
its soul leaves with a cloud
of dragonflies beyond
the Cedar River.

The cistern alongside the house
is full of rain. She drinks a ladle full
to take back what is

lost. Her husband's breathing
colors the night blue.
Herself astray, she curls
beneath his sleeping arm.

In the morning she tells him no
more than the eddy at the edge
of the river, or the silent
circling trout.

Erin Olds

Lost

That growing swell, infantine and minute
No bigger than the connecting of my cells
To yours and yours to mine, microscopic,
Pin-sized, growing slowly to small-orange size.

We watch you grow and as you do, we, took,
Grow into the parents we wish we knew how to be.
I count the days between hearing your heartbeats,
Pray for your aortas and chambers to form perfectly.

Your heart is in me and so I would have thought
That when it stopped beating I would have noticed.
Some monumental jerk should have shattered me.
I should have crumbled to the floor and wept.

Instead, I made Macaroni and Cheese and wondered if you would like it.
I imagined the orange sauce dying your toddler lips and hands
I would wash your grubby fingers and put you down for a nap,
Watch you tumble into heavy toddler-sleep after a sticky kiss.

I should have felt you leave.
But I spent the next seventeen days
Imagining a future that you, my son-or-daughter
Would never have and that I would never share.

Matthew Hohner

Psalm 40
for my birth mother on my fortieth birthday

I am listening online to a song no human has heard
before: a red giant's firelight rearranged into sound
waves, its pulses crossing the cold light years to earth.
It is the throbbing sound of blood pumping through veins,
the sound inside a womb of a mother I have never known.

Was it the same for you forty years back, my birth
a sound you'd never heard? A hard sound sharper
than scalpels, cutting a hole in you the size of God,
pulling you apart at the atoms, the silence
afterward only forgiveness could fill?

It is said that red stars are largest just before
collapsing in on themselves, a strange sort of birth
of the absence of light, where time bends and slows
to a stop, where nothing escapes, not even love.

I am listening to an old song
last heard through placenta and bone
from a warm universe long since forgotten
except by you—the pain of that day, the sound
of a black hole forming in your heart
where a son used to be.

Nancy Gerber

Little Scar

Scars on the earth and the bottom of the sea. Scars on the body and the soul. Scars visible and invisible. Scars of death and life, self-inflicted, accidental. The scar on your placenta.

When I was pregnant, I started to bleed in the first trimester. I had never been pregnant, and I did not understand the danger. An ultrasound, bed rest for a week, the doctor said everything was okay. Okay? I did not know anything about pregnancy. The bleeding stopped.

When you were born, there was a struggle. The umbilical cord was wrapped around your neck. You were in distress. You nearly choked to death. They wanted to C-section but couldn't: you were already in the birth canal. Between forceps and suction they pulled you through.

Then the placenta. The doctor held it in front of me and pointed to a thin, jagged line. "Here's the sign of bleeding ," he said. "The placenta tore and healed itself. This is the scar of the healing."

I was tired. I heard your cries and wanted to hold you. I did not want to see a purple, bloodied thing dangled before me like a piece of meat. I did not study the cicatrice that sealed your fate and gave you to me. I did not thank God for the healing.

I am older now and wiser. I remember that scar and trace its jaggedness. I thank God for the miracle. Bless the scars, I say. Bless all the scars.

Mary Jo Balistreri

Remembering With a Last Line by Neruda

Smoke smudges the air.
I lean on the rake
and watch Sam wobble
across the lawn, small legs pumping hard,
unsteady, but Eden in his heart. He falls,
begins again until he reaches
his brother's hill of leaves, cascade of gold
from Zachary's hands,
where he stands king of the mountain.

Zach encourages him to climb up, but Sam
keeps sliding down, all the time laughing,
delighted with this freedom, the crunch
of leaves under his new white shoes.

Finally content to sit at the bottom of the heap,
Sam lifts fistfuls of leaves, then releases
them to fall like confetti—into his blonde hair,
onto his sweater where they snag in the red airplane.

Leaf Man!
Sam shouts as he names
red
yellow
red
yellow

That time was like never, and like always.

for Sam (1997-2005) Zachary (1993-2007)

Marcia J. Pradzinski

In the House on Emerson

quiet comes every time I pass
        the place you sat watching
                videos on your blue gym mat.

the quiet

not the kind that stilled the air
                as we read *Jungle Book*,

not the kind loaded
        with patience – waiting
                for the school bus and your hugs,

not the quiet comfort
        of baby-warmth
                cuddled in my arms.

it is the quiet that blooms to silence,
        a voice lost that packs the house
                tight with emptiness.

Elvis Alves

For the mother who is still a mother even though she has lost a child

She says pray and I pray, pull words
from I do not know where,

remembering to say God, comfort, peace,
strength

But what I really want to say is rise, like
Jesus did Lazarus, and watch her tears
disappear

Make her days, years, better

But I cannot do as Jesus and so her baby
lies dead in front of me, in front of her,

silent as the moment before the world was
created

and the only thing I hear, and hope she hears,
is that may God give you comfort, peace, strength
to live these days, these years

dear mother.

Jane Frances Harrington

Moving Day

High tide at 1:52pm, the paper said. Almost that now. I've had to turn back twice for closed roads. You expect water in town, close to the bay, but not here on higher ground, on the way out.

I should know where I am, I say to no one, I should have paid attention to these bookshelves of neighborhoods growing around us. This one still has "For Sale" signs in front of slits of houses façade-abreast-façade, chimneys erect, waiting for arrivals. I peer through the blur to see the street name at an intersection, but it, too, is unfamiliar. To the left the water has filled all but a thin scar of macadam down the middle of the road, and I watch as a real estate sign is pulled into the torrent, leaving its post though its work isn't done. I turn right.

She used to take pictures downtown just after storms. A floody place, we called it once, honoring Pooh. At first her subjects were all serendipity, smiling kayakers plying the streets, but later she shifted her lens below the waterline, to the damage: the soggy stores, the wet dogs, the broken boardwalk. The things that felt the pressure beneath. I packed up those images early this morning. They're in a shoebox labeled "Photos Mel took, 1996-2008." Maybe they're on the seat next to me, but I'm not sure. I moved the boxes so many times to make them fit, as if laboring over one of our bewildering block puzzles—that one that falls apart in the end if you don't place every piece just so. I packed that, too, in a big box with all the games. Those I trusted to the movers, but not the photos, not the origami or the clay. Not the journals, those volumes that multiplied on the nightstand shelf, taboo for a mother to read—unless… and then, well, they whisper: Why didn't she read them? A mother should have known.

The car skids, hydroplanes momentarily, the boxes of things I don't want to forget and things I don't want to remember shift and creak. One topples, from the sound of it, but I don't take my attention from the wheel. I probably need new tires. Or maybe I should just stop driving this old car. Put it in a box and label it "The car Mel rode in…."

Here's a street I recognize, and I head again in the direction of the new apartment. I can barely see. Water fills my view faster than the beat of the wipers, faster than the flick of my eyelids. But if the tide finds me here, I'll will the car to stay afloat, to buoy on the relentless swell. Under me the damages will be swept off—the silence that stole laughter, slashes of innocence—gone as suddenly as they appeared. And I'll stay at the waterline. Dry-eyed.

Gabriella Burman

On Friday Nights

Lately, my four-year-old thinks she is old enough to strike the matches. On Friday evenings at sundown, when we light candles to usher in the Jewish Sabbath, she climbs onto the countertop, and grabs the slim box with chubby hands that resemble her oldest sister's.

Without fail, each week, she does this, and without fail, each week, her father and I admonish her that matches are dangerous, somehow not mastering, ourselves, the lesson to keep them out of her reach at the moment we take them out of the cupboard.

Every family has its variation of how the blessing is recited. Some light a pair of candles; some, as we do, light for the number of members of the family. Some recite the blessing in order of seniority; others, in unison. In traditional homes, only the women light; in others, the men participate. But the Hebrew words, whether sung or spoken, remain the same: Blessed are You, Lord our God, King of the universe, who has sanctified us with His commandments, and commanded us to light the Sabbath candles.

In our family, the blessing is sealed with a kiss.

This is how I was raised. As soon as Shabbat began, my sister and I stood by our mother's side as she lit her silver candelabra. It stood on a shining mirrored plate on a buffet in the dining room, in front of an octagonal mirror that reflected us, watching her. She placed her manicured hands over her eyes, and silently said the blessing, followed by a lengthy moment of quiet that indicated a dialogue with God. What she asked of Him, she never shared. When she was done, my sister and I each took our turn, and then she kissed us with great force. Shortly thereafter, we sat down to eat.

In my home, I bless five candles in the kitchen, atop a paper covered with Sabbath-themed stickers, stuck to a layer of protective, yet scratched, acrylic. It was a preschool present from Michaela, our oldest daughter, who died unexpectedly when she was five. I never added a silent prayer to God the way my mother does, but now, I offer up a silent "Fuck You."

This is especially true on the eves of Jewish holidays, which are also ushered in by candle lighting, and to which we add a second blessing thanking God for enabling us to "reach this occasion." The phrase sounds more powerful in Hebrew, no more so than when David Ben Gurion exclaimed it upon the establishment of the State of Israel, or when my grandfather, a survivor of Auschwitz, proclaimed it at my wedding. To me, now, that second blessing is, simply, offensive. I thank no one for arriving at this moment; I feel scorched by my daughter's death, and have neither the envy for, nor the capacity to emulate, those who retain faith after catastrophe.

But this is my heritage. To have created a Jewish home after the Holocaust was a source of pride for my Zaide, as we called him, and it has been paramount to my mother, who refers to the imperative every chance she gets. It is all she can do for her parents, I believe, after what they endured, their forearms branded with numbers, their dreams blazing forever thereafter, despite the prescriptions they took.

The truth is, when I was a child, I loved being a Jew, the stories of our patriarchs, the exodus from Egypt, the fall of the walls of Jericho. I took pride in speaking Hebrew, mastering text, and feeling completely secure, as when I walked into a synagogue during a college semester in Paris, opened a prayer book in the sanctuary, and immediately felt at home.

And even when, as an adult, I became more skeptical of religion, coming to view it as a man-made construct, I continued to observe Shabbat and to keep kosher. When Adam and I married, we agreed to raise our children the way we had been raised. If, playing out the quintessential Jewish parental nightmare, they ultimately reject our lifestyle, we reasoned, at least, they'll know what they're leaving.

Michaela, who had cerebral palsy and could not speak, told us in her way that she enjoyed Shabbat, her eyes widening along with the rise in a melody, and "mmming" at the cold grape juice she tasted after Adam blessed the wine, and I suspect this would have gone on forever. While it is too soon to tell with the more emotional Maayan, I am doubtful that Ayelet, our middle daughter, will ever rebel. Ayelet's heart flutters with devotion that is absent in my own heartbeat; her soul shines through deep, brown eyes. She loves God even more than her parents, she says, "because He gave me you!" and she truly believes, at age six, that God is responsible for everything, and that we must thank Him every day.

She is the one who leads us in blessing on Friday nights. Standing at a safe distance from the flames, her hair swinging like a drape, she covers her eyes and sings in Hebrew, using a tune she learned at school. Maayan copies her moves, and sings along in a voice that would be lovely if she didn't scream so much. I accompany them; if I am too quiet, they shout, "Louder, Mommy!" After we're done, we grin and hug like happy apes, and then the girls return to their cartwheels.

I linger a moment, before setting the table with challah, silver goblets, and what will always be the wrong number of plates. I gaze at the passport-sized pictures of each of my daughters, which I've set next to my own candelabra. For a fine-haired moment, I take small comfort in knowing there is something I continue to do which still involves the number five. I will always, always light five candles.

7.

Melanie Sweeney

Eviction

That winter when the days quit,
short and bruised, the skinny aspens
quaking under burdens of snow,
I saw dead birds everywhere.
Big black ravens whose oil-slick
wings splayed in the wind, beady
yellow eyes disbelieving a sky
the same gray as the shoveled
driveways where they fell.

My mother in her burgundy robe
sank into the snow-covered step.
Another notice taped to the door,
corners flapping. The feathers are stiff.
She flicks her ash and tells me,
Don't touch that, it's ridden.

Donna Katzin

Woman's Work
for Rosinal Tshisevhe

It took all her strength,
beyond the years of cooking pap for her husband,
six children, to dream for decades
of leaving her own signature
in the soil.

It took all her courage
(and a "token of respect")
to ask the headman
for twenty hectares to plant
an invisible crop in dry dirt.

It took all her nerve to seek
advice from the white farmer --
baas of brothers, sisters,
neighbors -- to defend her tomatoes
from the army of worms.

Where now will she find
the fortitude to face the banker,
tame costs of chemicals, power,
plant butternuts and okra, rebirth the business
of seeding life in this hard land?

Wendy Vardaman

Genesis, the Movie

One hundred people wake up one morning in a cozy house with enough bathrooms, bedrooms, kitchens, couches to accommodate all of them. They know it's the first day of their lives, but not why they're there. Life is good. Babies are born painlessly within 24 hours of mating and grow up in the next 24-hour period without parenting. Fresh food appears in cupboards. The refrigerator hums along and doesn't need cleaning. The dogs don't shed.

So why isn't everyone happy? Hard to say. By the end of Week 1, after the population has soared, although there is still an abundance of clean towels, hot water and everyone's favorite flavors of ice cream, little cliques have started to form with special words and jokes that only some people know. Everyone agrees: Cain's a little odd. *Notice how he doesn't make eye contact? And he never comes to the volleyball games.* Abel, on the other hand, is, well, *able*: sporty, good-looking, funny.

Their mother says, *Cain doesn't apply himself to anything. Abel's so friendly.* Their dads have nothing to add or subtract to that. Cain keeps to himself. Never plays catch. Has a little notebook that he writes in constantly. Goes on walks alone. Studies lichens & seashells. And Abel? He likes basketball, plays guitar. Shoots looks at his girlfriends when Cain walks by. Starts moving Cain's stuff around, just for fun.

S'up bro? he asks. Raises an eyebrow. High fives a friend.

Theta Pavis

The Bloodbath

Everyone is confused.
The birds at the unseasonable
Weather, and me at
Myself wanting to watch
The birds flying through the near
Winter wreck of our backyard.

The neighbors seem confused, their
American flag wrapped and ratty
Around the pole, the dark lines
Of a tree running skyward past
Its sagging red remnant.

And the skyline from here, it's half
Clouded, half sun-streaked with
December rays, through which
The unfinished Freedom Tower
Stands stabbing at nothingness.

I am confused just looking at it. I am
Confused that the needle you pushed in
To me didn't hurt the first time, but did
The second. And about what the
Doctor said; I don't have that straight.

I'm confused about the money, why
The hospital chapel wasn't better cared
For, how to avoid unpleasant conversations
And what to say when my sister says she
Wishes she were dead.

I'm confused about the fiscal cliff and
Magazine clips that do away with the
Need to reload.

Kristin Procter

Burst

I
There is a skill of precision required in judging the right moment to twist the tap, and stop the flow of water stretching the bulbous balloon to its limit. Too little liquid and the ammunition will roll, dry and harmless, belly up in the grass – dud. Too much pressure and the little rubber ring that kisses the tap will be torn from its pregnant womb, launching the attack on yourself – spurt.

II
In the eggshell tub, she floats her moon belly back over her knees to hero's pose, head tipped to the sky, eating piano snowflakes with her persimmon cheeks and tomato tongue. She beckons her baby with body and breath. She opens; her fingers expand around the curve of his collapsible skull, as he breaks to the surface, erupting from water, to water, to arms.

III
Martha Stewart dismantles pomegranates online. She slices the sphere into two lobes, each of which in turn she cradles in her hand before swiftly striking the flesh with a large wooden mixing spoon. She insists this is not spanking, but as the tender red insides fall into a pile on the table, I can't help but wonder how exactly Martha spanks.

IV
Dangling fingers like bait in a fish farm, she trawls for shimmer in her drawer of delicates. She pushes aside armpit high monthly mom pants. Her pinkie hooks a long forgotten key lime G-string, with a lace ruffle and history that quicken her pulse. She slips off her track pants and wiggles back into her sexuality. In front of the full length mirror, it is difficult to say which pops first, her eyes or the undergarments' over-extended waistband. Either way, her hip stings and her ankles have been swallowed by a polyester green tree snake.

V
Emerging overnight, through the newly defrosted soil, crocus sprouts stretch green armpits, to beckon spring. She halts her senseless massacre of ants, to inspect this new growth, bends from the waist, over her thick toddler thighs, Ah look. Little fishies opening them's mouths, she coos. She lifts, balances precariously on one leg, with a sparkle-infused foot grenade poised to flatten the fins on this delicate crocus-fish. Then the wind changes; So does her mind. She kneels to the ground, fish kisses.

VI

I drive in a daze, oblivious to the presence of 5 year old ears wrapped around every word bleeding from the radio. People are dead. Sneaker-clad limbs litter the finish line of the marathon that invites the world to Boston. "What is shrapnel" he asks, and as if on cue, the radio advises the home cooked bombs spewed metal fragments, nails and ball bearings. The number of injured grows, like temperature rising. I turn on the air conditioner, grateful that for now, his questions start with what and not why.

Emily R. Blumenfeld

In triptych breath and silk

across maps of ancient wisdom, inside labyrinths of breath, within circles of arms, with womblike warmth of open palms, by the sacred sake of nurture, for a lullaby's caress, for silk, for dreams

under the moon before a sun, in a room on the edge, in eye view across eye contact, by herself for others, for some life for some lives, for sometime for all time, within held breath, within silk confine

above land mines under drones, after genocides after guns, inside footsteps of steel, inside gardens of grief, inside her spirit inside her flesh, within speechless breath, across umbilical cords of braided silk

Meredith Trede

Jarheads

After 12 weeks the hatchlings at Parris Island
all look alike, shaven heads, gaunt faced,
thick necked, stride alike in bulldog cadence:

fifty-four hours in simulation of war, wrung
through a Crucible, lines of warriors now
in perfect formation on the Parade Ground.

We strain to find our boy among these men.
At a social event an acquaintance asked,
Where did he grow up? Never supposing

our middle class haven, where others do
the heavy lifting. As we look for the one who
tucks in his little brother with a kiss and

whispered, *Honey*: platoon leader busted,
for being too nice, consensus won't work
in the trenches. There. He's striding to us.

Claudia Van Gerven

The Boy
-after the sculpture G.I. Joey by Caroline Douglas

When does he slip out of your worried pockets
twisted blood cord no longer forwarding
his night sighs? When is his air

safe to breathe
before you breathe it?

You have asked here   and here   and here
where are we?   Which war is this?

Ordinary red sky, small birds wheeling, shattering
into trees. You are a beginner in this old skin
crackling fierce as plutonium.

You scan the coming darkness, lazar
onslaught of days, their dangers crying out
on the evening news.

It's been years since he rode
exultant and terrified
on your monstrous monster
slaying hip.

He has fallen from the grip
of your frayed apron, your corded
competent hands,
his scars knotted anagrams.

He bleeds long distance. Your doorway
has been disappeared. You must turn
the porch light off.

8.

Susan Fox

Piano Recital at the Old Folks' Home

Sixty silent heads respectful –
Chopin not even a memory for most
but respect, they remember.
Then Malagueña,
then light in blear eyes
        my mother's hands
                dancing
                        faster
      the wheelchair next to hers
              rocking in time.
The very old lady smiles.
Her almost old daughter strains for music.
Malagueña calms to Bach
        someone begs hoarsely for Ave Maria
            I lean toward one pair of fidgeting hands:
"It's almost over now."

John Warner Smith

Songs We Never Heard

Why, in her dying days,
did my grandmother thank us
for listening? We hadn't heard
the dew-drip taps of tears
that dropped to her pillow,

the thunder rumbling in her womb,
nor the curious soliloquy of cuss
and prayer that seethed through
her midnight-gritting teeth
as she paced the dusty hallways

dragging her feet with the burden
of hungry babies at her breasts
and Jim Crow on her shoulders.
We hadn't heard the soft rattle
of beads streaming through

her coarse hands that ached
as she prayed and bled
as she pushed a plow
or spun the sewing wheel.
When the trumpet blew, we

gathered freshly-cut flowers,
spread like a mort cloth of silk,
scented of frankincense and myrrh,
and walked her path, worn
with the weariness of living.

Recounting her days, we hummed
her Sunday songs in the fading
glow of her last sunset.
But we never heard the blues
our old black mothers knew.

John Minczeski

She Became

Maggie
Breath bar under her nose
slumped in a chair gazing out the window

She never said what she looked at
not the past
that bend in the river
a stump drifting downstream

Kicking off covers
tugging at her gown
the air superheated

her lungs saturated
her veins traffic jams
and it was always rush hour

Maggie
Sweaters and slacks in drawers
a coat she'd never wear again
Morphine Maggie

and *Morning Maggie*
the weather channel blaring
Doubting Maggie
looking out the window

waiting for her train
taking so long to arrive

would she like dinner?
Maggie wanting toast
dipped in coffee
soft boiled egg

The laying-on of hands
A priest

pinning the miraculous medal of Mary
to her sleeve

Tough-as-nails Maggie
sixty-three pounds
and not giving a whistler's damn
if it set the world record

Gerard Sarnat

Once we were enemies. Now she believes

I'm her father, reborn
    wiser, kinder.

Mom rests her head in my lap.

Issa M. Lewis

My mother's hair

started falling out last year in patches. I tell her
she could tattoo it back on. We take a step,
a small step into knowing that she's unraveling
like an unfinished hem. A little sass, a little irony might
keep it together, if she had MOTHER inked on there—
I'd always know where to find her.
That, and how her laughter floats on tears.

She is knitted in well-worn fibers—
lovely soft, but fraying slowly where flaws
in the fabric were hidden, dropped stitches
we did not see. Loose threads web
around the eyes, lightly around the lips' edge.

With the gentlest needle, I would sew
all the pieces together, thread into the cracks and tug
with thumb and forefinger until the sides kiss.

                But there is no needle,
no thread fine or strong enough to make those seams.

My fingers only fumble to draw her together,

                    knit a web large enough to catch us both.

Lesléa Newman

In The ICU

my mother is awake and not awake
my mother is asleep and not asleep
my mother is alive and not alive

the clock is moving and not moving
the monitor is beeping and not beeping
the nurse is coming and not coming

time is passing and not passing

my mother is seeing and not seeing
my mother is hearing and not hearing
my mother is breathing and not breathing

I am seeing her face and not seeing her face
I am hearing her voice and not hearing her voice
I am squeezing her hand and not squeezing her hand

I am beside her and beside myself

I am an orphan and I am not an orphan
I am a daughter and I am not a daughter
I am a child and I am not a child

her daughter
her child

Kyle Potvin

Instructions to the Youngest Child

Guard closely your mother's broach with the gold petals and birthstone-tipped
        pistils,
her crystal flutes, hand etched and paper thin,
and her antique armoire assembled without nails.

You may discard her painted figurines but not the ornaments
she placed on the five Christmas trees decorating your family home.

Today, pack up her pristine suits for someone else to wear.

Sift through the letters your father wrote to her in his elegant script, saved
in a decoupage box by her bed.

Find the green pincushion she wore on her wrist when she hemmed your
communion gown. Marvel that the straight pins stayed in place so long.

Toss the stack of old birthday cards but protect the album
carrying your life story behind its plastic pages.

Press your fingers in the dry dirt of her once thriving African violets.
Water the soil and watch it darken with a richness you haven't seen in years.

In the kitchen, inhale the sugary sweetness of the empty cookie tin.
Claim the wooden spoon, the sifter and the measuring cups she baked with
        all your life.

Save her jewelry box for your sister
and the inlaid wood table from Germany for your brother.

Your grandmother's wedding ring is yours already, given years before
by your mother, who shared your need for such things.

Patricia Behrens

Apology to My Mother

I am sorry I lost the Girard-Perregaux watch
you gave me for college graduation,
the one time you gave the gift you wanted,
not the cheaper thing that Father thought was just as good.

I am sorry I never gave you a Pendleton skirt
that you could lift from folded tissue paper
in a gift-wrapped box, but only the material to make one.

I am sorry I left the Aran Islands sweater you knitted on a bus.

I am sorry that coming out of anesthesia, I asked you to leave
the room, the day I had my wisdom teeth removed.

I am sorry I didn't know you had my picture in your wallet
until after you died.

I am sorry that we left your grave unmarked for thirty years
because Father wanted a gravestone only after he died, too.

I am proud that, finally, when we bury him, we put your name first.

"I worked in John Lewis baby department for twenty years."

Hester Jones

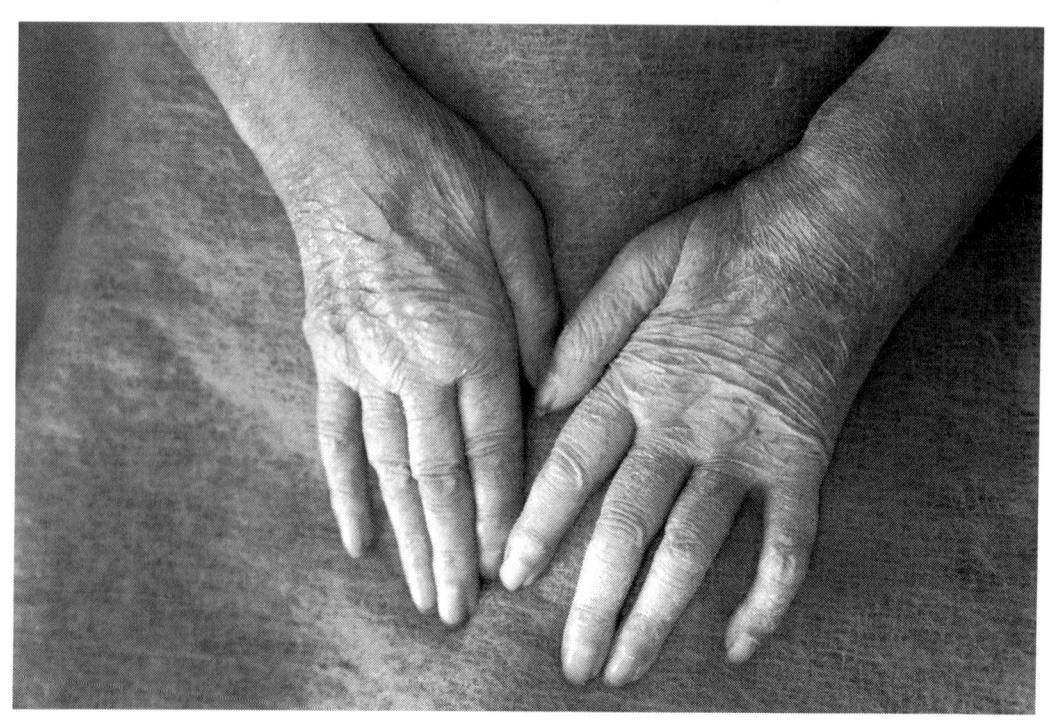

"I used to knit a lot, socks, we used to have sheep, take wool and knit it."

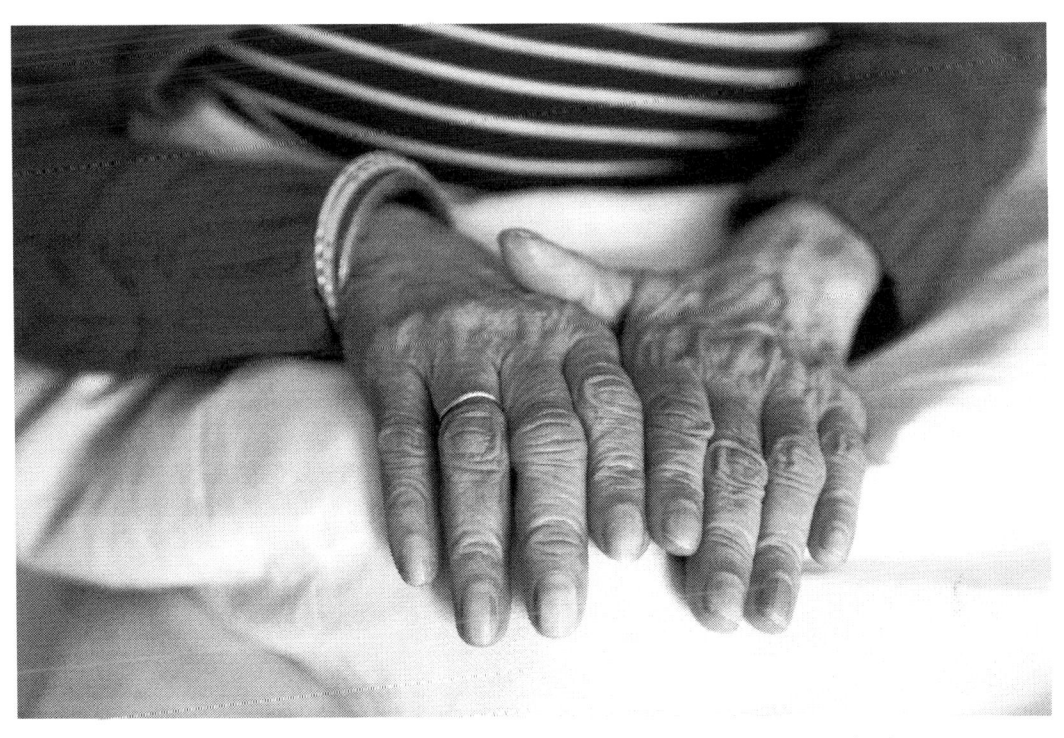

"I was a telephone operator."

"I used to work in Harrods in the confectionary department."

9.

Elaine Handley

Matrilineal

The way she pats dough, throws
crumbs to birds, pulls hair
back to snake down her back
her hands red raw.

The grace of hip and calf
at the clothesline careful
trace of red on lips
before answering the door.

Vanilla, lemon oil, vinegar, soap
Spools of thread, dust cloths, thimble,
lint and string, the unpaid gas bill--

part of my lost life in her apron pockets.

Stories stirred like soup with secret
ingredients parables at dinner warnings
at bedside the same voice milking
the diurnal air lament
of mourning dove repeating, repeating
shadow by the night door
at the window eyes knitting worry.

Claudia D. Hernández

Años Dorados
A ti, madre

Hoy vuelvo al nido
en busca
de tu conciencia.

Rendida caigo
sobre las tusas de tu petate,
buscando consuelo —

mi cuerpo
ha destrozado mi
alma en lluvia.

Tu sabes bien,

que lo que busco
no es beberme
tus palabras,

sino empaparme
en el vigor
de tu matriz.

Yo sé muy bien,

que lo que busco
en ti, es esa mirada que me
descose las venas enterradas.

Solo tu logras soldar
mi nervio perenne
de guerrera en flor.

Golden Years
A ti, madre

Today, I return
to the nest in search
of your wisdom.

Exhausted, I lay on your
petate of hay
hungry for comfort —

my body
has shattered my soul
into rain.

And you know so well,

that what I seek in you
is not to drink
your words,

but to immerse myself
in the vigor
of your womb.

And I know so well,

that what I seek in you
is that gaze, the one that
unstitches my hidden veins.

Only you can weld
my perennial nerve
of a blooming warrior.

Arlene Weiss

Miss Tessie

My mother noticed it as soon as I started to walk. I was a dancer! As soon as I heard music coming out of our antique Stromberg-Carlson (which took up most of our large living room), I would jump up and start to dance. By the time I was about ten years old, I was dancing to Artie Shaw, Benny Goodman, Kay Keyser and his College of Musical Knowledge…until, finally, my mother convinced my father that it would be a truly great shame ("actually a crime") to let any more time go by. She talked my father into it-- "Arlene Sonya must have dancing lessons!" But where was one to find a dancing teacher in East Islip, where the entire population wasn't much over 5000? Our little town barely existed through the Depression. Not only would it be next to impossible to find a good dance teacher, but how could we afford it? But leave it to my mom-- she herself had a beautiful singing voice and loved all kinds of dance and music. Leave it to my most resourceful mother. After quite a search, she did find someone, Miss Tessie. Miss Tessie was a former Broadway show girl who had seen better days but was still very, very lovely. She told my mother that the cost would be one dollar for a half-hour lesson. Of course, Miss Tessie had no idea that my mother had only about one dollar a day to feed our growing family of five.

Another a problem was that Miss Tessie's husband – who looked and acted more like a Nazi Storm Trouper than a human being – owned a Texaco gas station way east on Sunrise Highway on Long Island, 'way out in the boondocks'. Miss Tessie and her husband lived (miserably I am sure) in the two or three small rooms in back of their gasoline station, but there, at the top of the stairs in the attic, Miss Tessie had cleverly fixed up a dance studio.

Alas, it was my poor father who had to drive me every Monday night to Miss Tessie's. After all, gas cost money. But the worst of it was that Miss Tessie's husband was a brute. I hated having to face him every week – but when I went up the stairs to Miss Tessie's studio, all thoughts of his disgustingly fat face faded away.

After my first lesson, Miss Tessie told me that I danced very gracefully, and my routine would go over big. I was so happy. My first assignment was to learn the steps to an old-time, turn-of-the-century song. When my lesson was over, I jumped into the car and told my father that I had big, big news, but really he didn't much care. When I got home, I ran into the house screaming that I was going to be in a show. Best of all, I would be performing to the legendary "Alice Blue Gown" at the annual meeting of the Moose!

I practiced hard and earnestly. I didn't want to embarrass Miss Tessie and all her grown-up friends who would surely be there that night. I was anxiously awaiting dancing for grown-ups. Miss Tessie, ever so resourceful, made me a beautiful pink tutu that fitted me perfectly.

The night of the final rehearsal, as I ran up the stairs, I realized that Miss Tessie was about to receive a surprise. The fact was that a few days before, the dentist had put braces on my teeth. When I got to the top of the stairs Miss Tessie, after welcoming me warmly, suddenly gave me another look and this look was not funny. The woman was simply horrified. "Arlene, Arlene, I am sorry, darling, but there is no way you can be in the show tomorrow. I am sorry, but I simply cannot allow it." I almost died on the spot. "Why… what, what is it Miss Tessie?" "Why, Arlene, you will be right in front of the audience – you must realize that there is no stage - and you've got those – those – those things on your teeth. The audience will see that you are wearing BRACES."

After that, it was inescapable. I was to be ignored, stigmatized, shamed, and humiliated.

I told my father to take me right home. He didn't even ask me why. As I walked into our kitchen, my mother was washing the dishes. "Why Arlene, baby, what happened? " When I sobbed out my story, she ripped off her apron and ran for her coat. About 20 nervous minutes later, who should march into Tessie's studio but my mother.

I was back in the show.

And, to this day, I remember the lyrics to Alice Roosevelt Longworth's charming little tune, " My Sweet Little Alice Blue Gown."

Elisa A. Garza

Why Stieglitz Photographed O'Keeffe's Hands

Because careful petals
suggest the whole.

Because red hills are the sun
in muted sky.

Because a day becomes
a night and thus, goes on.

Felice Aull

My Mother's Power

is so great
years after she is dead
that seconds pass
before I startle to catch myself
speaking to her inside my head,
left to cast about--no one else
quite right for my news.

Cheryl Boyce-Taylor

Then On Friday's
After Robert Hayden's Those Winter Sunday's

Then on Friday's
her work week finally done
my mother came home
after scrubbing floors
on hands and knees

I should have thanked her   my lips to her soap logged hands
I should have thanked her

Friday's I'd wake to
Jesus loves me this I know
Mom's voice supported by the melody of pots and pans
smells of molasses and hot oatmeal on the stove
I'd scoot back under covers fearing she'd ask for help

I should have thanked her
filled the jug with warm bubbling milk
fetch the butter from the fridge
I should have thanked her

instead of frown and pout
about the faded coat
that was not fancy
the sneakers not real Keds

I should have thanked her my lips to her cheek
now I know   now I know.

10.

Pat Falk

Her Words

My mother said it doesn't matter if a woman comes or not.
It does, though, for a man—a backup of his sperm
will make his balls ache, he will get sick.
It seemed that women had to suck, blow, spread their legs,
push, pull, prod, do whatever was demanded
to disgorge the swollen manhood.
I imagined backed-up rivers, tiny fish trampled at the delta,
plankton turned to stone, to pebbles hard and raging.

Now my mother's old and sick and dying.
I wonder if she ever truly lived—given her take on love.
I wish her well. I wish her peace. But most of all
I wish she'd take that pack of lies back into the grave with her.
Had I believed her (but how could I believe her?)
maybe I'd have loved her and her weird and wicked ways;
I learned instead to love myself,
to live in cool blue darkness, on fire and alone.

Priscilla Atkins

Candy Store

The afternoon your mom gave us some money
to go to the Five-and-Ten and buy a treat
and after a half-hour dithering, we trotted back
with a package of raspberry licorice,
from her prone position in the sunny grass
she raised up on her elbows, scrunched her face
and announced, "Lick-o-reesh?" as in: *You've got
to be kidding; given a choice, who in the heck
would come up with that?* In the same way, the day,
years later, over the phone, you came out of the closet,
I can hear her mind's mouth gape. "Ho-mo-sect-chil?"
something like a too-bright sun watering her eyes,
silence clocking a slow ten before more brain
molecules kicked in: *Who'd go to the candy
store and come home with that?*

P.A. Pashibin

My mother's finger

Lorraine's finger attaches itself
to my right hand. Powerful digit.
All knowing. Invasive.

Stabs at sky, thrust and parry.
Pokes at shoulders. Wags in faces
of strangers. Of lovers.

Don't try to argue with this finger --
dancing, a cobra waiting to strike.
Her judgment, its venom.

Hers is a finger that gives no pleasure,
never felt suckling, touched no velvet.
Keeps guard above the waist.

Kathryn Kysar

The Burden

> "I remember being pregnant with my first child and still not knowing where the baby was going to come from,' said Margarita Villanueva, 59, who has seven children, 15 grandchildren, and three great grandchildren."
> *Minneapolis Star and Tribune*, Sunday, June 19, 2005

My mother only showed me
how to pin on the rag
to my underwear. Now my stomach
grows, and I am filled
with fear: how will this baby get out?
Will my belly explode? Will the doctor
slice me open like a melon? Will
my belly button, already stretched
tight, pucker an opening, a vortex
for the baby to crawl through,
just as the Huichols say the first
people crawled up through the earth?

I am filled with questions:
I cannot ask the doctor, whose
large white cold hands touch me
quickly, brusquely, in front of the
silent nurse. I cannot ask my mother,
who turns toward the white fish
with lemon she cooks for tacos,
too embarrassed to speak.
I pray to the Virgin Mary, a mother,
but was Jesus born the earthly way?
My cousins in el campisinos may know,
but did God make women
like a cow, pig, or perro?

I wonder if this is Eve's curse,
our fate for her temptation:
we are forbidden to know
how to relieve ourselves of these
burdens of babies, these strange,
ungodly fruits inside our flesh.

Patrice Boyer Claeys

Hunger

Growing up, I never
saw my mother eat
save for covert cramming
of cold potato
clumps from littered
plates, her back
turned, facing the iron
sink in isolation
as she gnawed bones
slated to be dumped.

I never felt my mother's
love, save for sharp
corners of ironed
hankies snapped
into purses clutched
in matching gloves, the raking
scratch of plastic teeth
untangling wayward strands,
and sheets aggressively
tucked in confining creases.

What a hollow craving
for the cushioning lap,
the gentle cupping
of the quivering chin, the pause
to recognize in hesitant eyes
a hunger unabated, even
as she dusted maraschino
flecks with flour, blood red
slivers speckling the angel
cake we would later devour.

Laura Madeline Wiseman

The Right Size

Leather boots, tight black skirt, button-down tops—
she's getting ready again, a slip swirls mid-thigh,
foundation softens the lines and wrinkles,
curlers in hair, their metal pins tight to her skull.
We watch her, pretend to clean the kitchen, and linger
in the living room before the TV as the pantyhose shine,
the eye shadow glitters, the wet mascara wand sparkles.
She shimmies into a skirt, taunt on her narrow thighs,
slides into a black top open to her throat, slips on
low heeled boots that reveal her delicate ankle bones—
the right size—Any man will fuck you when you're skinny.

When I begin to lose weight, I feel sexy, lovable,
like eyes on me as I walk in smaller and smaller jeans
and in tiny tops, light-headed, giddy without food.
When I don't eat, my hipbones jut like a model,
like my mother, rib bones visible, no fat dimples,
no belly sag from three babies, no muffin top.
I am as trusting that I can control my life by diet.

Was she ever the right size? Maybe sometimes
at the end of the date, a man's hands on her
breasts, his fingers inside her mouth, the release
from White Rain hairspray, ½-Price Store clothes.
For just one moment the world saying, yes.
Yes, not eating is worth it, worth this.

Jessica Feder-Birnbaum

Buttercrunch

Standing online at Staples with her husband and daughter
The mother sees clear plastic boxes of high end candy
Wrapped in polyurethane were salted caramels, organic gummy bears, and buttercrunch
The mother remembers when she stayed with cousins - upstate without her parents
They were greeted at the candy shop by rainbow lollypops and peanut butter fudge
Vats of simmering chocolate and vanilla extract perfumed the air
White smocked ladies offered tastes of raspberry jelly beans and buttercrunch squares
Buttercrunch with its crispy toffee center, milk chocolate coat and sprinkle of almonds
Was the grandmother's favorite
The mother took out two dollars of saved up allowance
The buttercrunch was wrapped in a white box tied with a red ribbon
The mother imagined hugs and kisses and eating buttercrunch with the grandmother
When the grandmother came to pick the mother up, the mother handed her the box
At first the grandmother smiled
Then she opened the box and cried out
How dare you buy me buttercrunch – buttercrunch is my weakness
It will make me get fat
The mother learned her lesson
Candy and cookies made people weak and fat
But cottage cheese and grapefruits made people skinny and strong
The daughter is outraged – and tells the mother to confront the grandmother
The mother shakes her head
The grandmother was a thirty nine year old woman petrified of a piece of candy
Who passed down the fear to the mother
The mother now understands that she can buy a box of buttercrunch
Not wrapped in polyurethane at Staples, but freshly made at a candy shop
And she can sit down with the grandmother now eighty-one and her daughter now eighteen with nothing to fear
And they can each have a piece or two of butter crunch
With a cup of tea, some kisses, and some hugs

Jacqueline Doyle

Summer Fruits

I can't remember much in the way of good home cooking from my nineteen-fifties New Jersey childhood. I mostly remember the tension at the supper table.

We lived in a ramshackle three-story house built in 1914, and my father was always engaged in ambitious repairs and renovations. The kitchen was crowded and chaotic, half remodeled, with cabinets in two different colors and no countertops along one wall. We ate dinner together at a small black-and-gray-patterned formica table pushed against the unfinished cabinets. There was barely room for four plates.

My mother was an indifferent homemaker. We ate overcooked meats: stringy pot roast, tough pork chops (my father insisted that pork be well cooked because of the danger of worms), chicken breasts wrapped in bacon and baked until they were dry. We ate fish every Friday in those pre-Vatican II days—usually halibut that my father picked up at the fish market in Hoboken on his way home from work, a thick grayish-white fish broiled until it was leathery, served with minute rice and canned peas.

My parents bickered nonstop through dinner. I can't recall what they fought about, only the raised voices, the dissatisfaction that filled the room like steam from a simmering pot that leaves the windows and walls dripping with moisture. My brother and I ate poised on the edge of our seats, trying not to listen. The night I recall most vividly was when my father's anger boiled over and he hurled a full plate of food at the sink, leaving a dent in the stainless steel backsplash to mark the occasion.

There was one childhood meal I loved, however. Perhaps it's not surprising that no cooking was required. Imagine a warm summer night on the screened-in back porch off the kitchen. It's already dark outside, and the sky is full of stars, the Milky Way a hazy white blur in the blue-black heavens. Fireflies wink in the back yard.

The four of us are sitting at the round porch table in the dark, the only light spilling out from the partly closed back door to the kitchen. In the center of the table is an enormous white plastic bowl of fruit salad—diced fresh fruits from one of the summer produce stands in nearby Rockaway Valley: watermelon, cantaloupe, honeydew, blackberries, strawberries, green grapes. My brother and I have been playing outside all day, tramping through the woods on Pollard Road, swimming at Birchwood Lake, running through the rotating sprinkler in the back yard, the dog nipping at our heels.

The night is full. No one says anything. There is a sort of hushed reverence in the soft darkness, the silence. The fruits are so sweet on my tongue that I want the meal never to end.

Stephanie Feuer

Drumstick

The adults were downstairs. Their voices mingled with the smell of turkey and came up through the heating vent in my older cousin Mitchell's room. The windows of his room were all steamy. Outside the snow fell, perfect for sledding. We'd driven from New York to spend Thanksgiving with them in Scranton, Pennsylvania. It felt like nowhere.

We were inside because he didn't like to play outdoors with me, because, I suspected I could throw a ball harder and shoot baskets better and I was a girl and only 8. He'd want to play football. He was 13 and stronger, but if I got a chance to run, he'd say I cheated. Then I'd cry and he'd tell the adults I was a sore loser. The adults usually believed him. Sometimes I was a sore loser, but mostly he hurt me.

He asked me if I ever played doctor with my friends. I told I'd played with my neighbor Larry, that summer in the miniature log cabin that decorated my parent's suburban back lawn. Then Mitchell asked me to do something with him, a special game of doctor.

Why should I? I questioned him. His answer was the same answer he gave about mostly everything. "Because I lost a sister," he'd say and half-close his dark brown eyes. His sister, Lisa, was a year older than me and had died at 6 of encephalitis. I didn't really believe her death excused his behavior, but I couldn't argue with it.

It seemed an odd thing to do. It wasn't anything I'd heard of, and I thought I'd heard a lot because I'd spent so much time at the nursing home my father ran. I knew all about health conditions, catheters and cheating boyfriends from eavesdropping on the nurses. What Mitchell was talking about I hadn't heard of.

I stared at the molding. It was a red and white stencil my aunt had done herself. She was crafty like that, and a really good cook. Even my grandmother said she made the best version of the family stuffing recipe. I liked to cook, too, and longed to be in the kitchen with the good smells and women.

Mitchell grabbed me by the shoulder and pulled me towards him. He unzipped his pants, and with his hand at the back of my neck, pushed me towards his lap. My face rubbed against the navy blue carpet. It burned the skin of my cheek. There were red flecks in the carpet. Eraser residue. I struggled, but he was bigger. He held me down for a moment. It was hard to breathe.

"Suck like a lollipop," he told me. It was kind of squishy, not like anything I'd had in my mouth before. I didn't understand why this strange act was what he wanted so much, or why he got away with everything, just cause his sister had died.

I heard the wood stairs creak. I froze. Was this something I'd get in trouble for?

"Its turkey time," my father announced in a jovial voice, stopping on a step half way up the stairs.

I jerked at the sound of his voice. I must have hurt Mitchell, or maybe he was afraid of being caught. He pushed my head away, hard, slapped me, and zipped up his pants.

"He's hitting me," I said and started to cry. "Cry baby, cry baby," he sneered.

"Work it out, you two," my father said, no longer sounding so cheerful, "and come down to eat."

My uncle carved the beautifully cooked turkey, its juices escaping from its bronzed skin and puddling on the big wood cutting board. I took my seat at the table, next to Mitchell. My uncle asked my father and me if we'd like to share a drumstick.

"You take it," I told my father. "I don't have much of an appetite."

Electra Hunzeker

Sweet Valley

Elizabeth or Jessica? I don't remember which Wakefield twin your Barbie was when we played Sweet Valley, Angie, but I remember spending hours listening to Hit 105 and riding banana-seat bikes to Center 90 to buy makeup with our babysitting money. Then we'd turn up Whitney Houston and take off our ugly eighties glasses so we could transform ourselves from pudgy and pimples into absolutely divine. And we'd crimp our hair and your mom would yell at us—how we better not go outside looking like that—but if we were at my house, my mom wasn't around to care. I remember your neon yellow socks, Angie, and that I bought you a subscription to Seventeen for your birthday and how your house always smelled nicer than mine because your mom had all those baskets of potpourri.

I really should call you. My mom ran into your mom at Shopko a couple weeks ago. You're still there, right where you always were, only now you've had five babies. Five babies! I guess I heard about each one, and meant to send you a card each time, but you know how that goes.

I'm wondering what happened because one day there were two girls who were as close as twins and they spent their summers doing whatever they wanted. They sat on the deck wearing shorts and dangled their pale legs in the sun. They drank Tang and ate Chips Ahoy and recorded You Can't Do That on Television on the VCR so they could watch it over and over. They watched Showtime because they thought they were grown, and they watched cartoons because they were still girls. It doesn't seem like that long ago, but one of those girls had five babies and the other girl almost had one, but instead she got a Ph.D. It was the right choice, but sometimes she still cries over the loss of a life she'll never know, with soccer games and birthday parties and reading Goodnight Moon at bedtime.

So my mom says you're going to be a grandma, Angie. A grandma. I lied. I do remember which Wakefield twin you were: Jessica. The one I wanted to be. But you were my best friend, so I was willing to let you have all the fun.

Vicki Iorio

At 60

My sister confesses-
she hasn't listened to the Beatles since college,
since that winter day when her apartment
pushed out so much heat
it was either a bikini or skin

Her baby wouldn't stop crying
my sister couldn't stop crying
Yesterday didn't stop the crying

Sis turned off the stereo
packed up hope
switched to news radio

She confesses over birthday martinis-
                                        dirty
She confesses to me-
                  the dirty sister.

who forgives her every red pimento sin
                  every green heart floating in brine

Tsaurah Litzky

My Mother Told Me

My Mother told me it would be like this,
I would stumble on the stairs, or
go back down the hall on my way out
to see if I locked the door,
something I never did before.

*You better marry again before you lose
your looks, get too old*, she said.
You'll be frightened of being alone.

Not me, not me, never, I told her.

My ankles ache when I do yoga,
I assume frog pose, my knees creak,
I breathe deep, deeper, I need more air,
but I persevere, persevere.

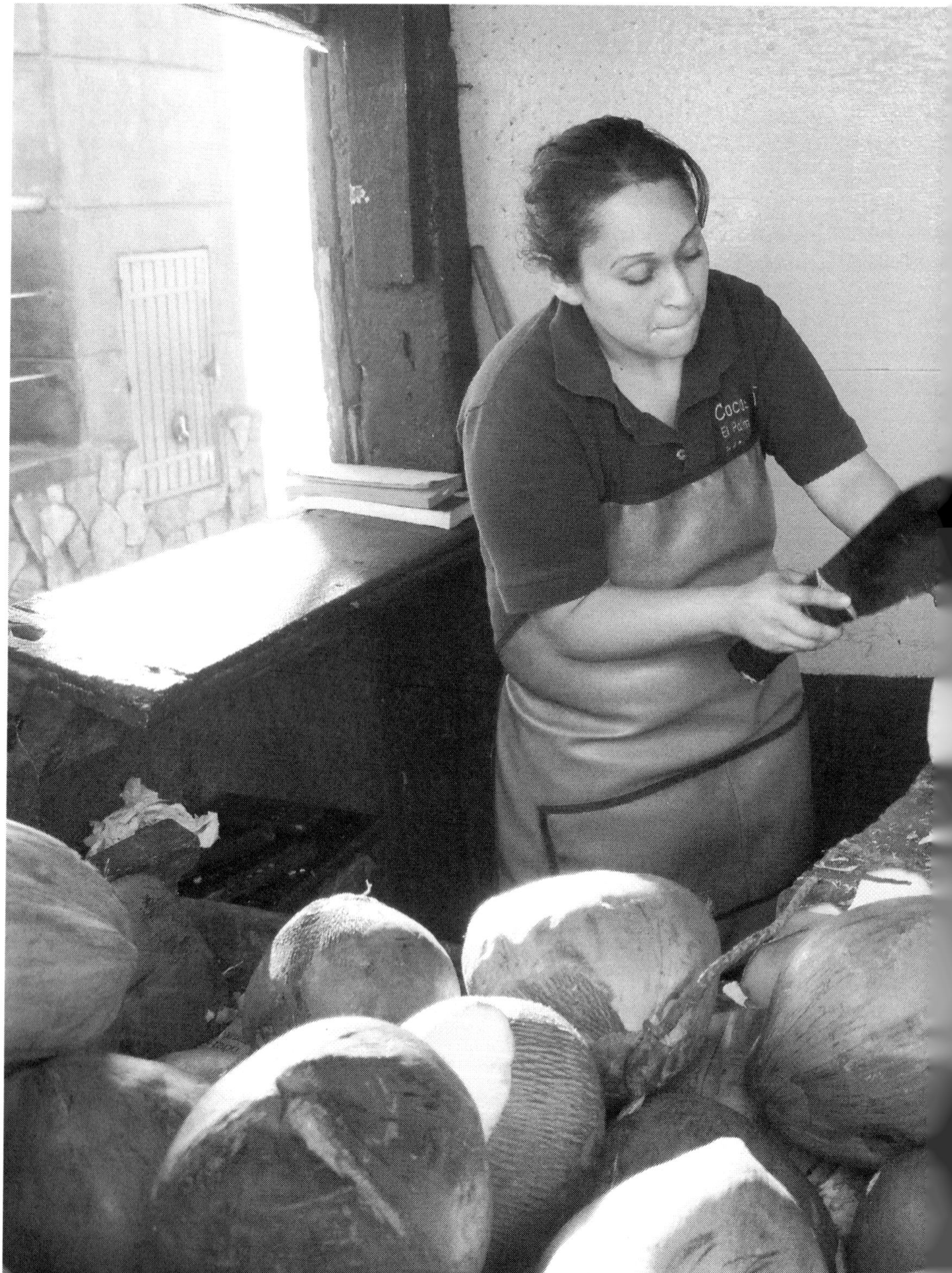

Claudia D. Hernández												In The Distance

11.

Caroline Beasley-Baker

fame/rise-fall-of-it (gertrude stein)

my pb-copy/
the-selected-writings
has yellowed — fallen-apart:

to-paraphrase —
nobody knows-it
'til everybody knows-

it?
ah/well —
little by little

my sacred emily
so-clearly-expressing-
something — we

begin again:
'rose-is-a-rose-is-a-rose'
— ah/well . . . 'till-it's-not?

Christine Swint

Number 1 1948

At Thanksgiving my freshman son unfurls
his sails—collages of plastic babies
tagged @99cents, bees swirling from
ovals reminiscent of skulls, narratives
of impastoed glyphs. He says the first time
he pinned his work to the board
a girl remarked, *These drawings look like
somebody locked himself in a room for a month
and painted his ravings on the walls.*
We go to the High Museum, where I admit
I prefer Matisse's domestic interiors,
that I enjoy tracing his wallpaper
to some logical conclusion, that Pollock
leaves me tense, out of breath, and he asks,
How do you feel about Number 1 1948?
                              Angry, I say.
But when we turn to Pollock's black dribbles,
we track one of his dodecaphonic arcs, and together
we drift toward a handprint, an anchor
at the edge of this kinesthetic sea.

Golda Solomon

is it art or laundry on a christmas day

dancing t-shirts all in a row
jimmied clothesline between industrial
hooks pining for summer lushness

wooden pins hold on tight to white
wet haynes shoulders
blanket the terrace

in small, medium and large
profile of her face silk screened
cropped wiry hair in purple

black outline of strong mouth
intense eyes and brow bleed
fuchsia and pink

this year's holiday gifts
in the making
twenty repeats of her face

julia's regatta in
her race to complete
and deliver before new years

we see art-in-process as we
turn the corner and look up
they billow and greet us

as the last rays of winter sun
dips down on the horizon
our neighbors see only laundry

Katrinka Moore

earth

shift of under-
brush, murmur
flicker — fox
in shadows

hidden behind conifers —
apple flowers

air

two owls fly, white
against the hemlocks —
one high, one low

tall grass waves
in the field, daisies
stir on the rise, tiny
ridges fan across
the pond — cattails shimmer
even when it's still

water

light fades, the boat
drifts, reflections
darken on the river

rainy night, frogs leap &
glow in the headlights

log bridge across
the stream — snapping
turtle

swallow dives, snags
a bug — perfect
circles ripple
to the banks

fire

full moon at solstice — we
can barely see the fireflies

Elizabeth Lara

Sacagawea

The child not yet born he sings to me
we are water / we are earth
his hands will scoop up the stars

I am far from my father's house
yet I dream the taste of ripe berries
and salmon swimming upstream

In winter I give birth
wolf prowls the prairie
the world is wind / is white

In April we set out on the river
by August we have crossed
the mountains

West of Lemhi Pass
the Shoshone Chief
rides with his warriors

He is my brother Cameahwait
I cry out as he dismounts and says
You are alive / A fine son

This morning I made
new moccasins
and added beads to my dress

In my hair I placed
an eagle feather
a great bird soaring
on pillars of air

Zoë Ryder White

In Brooklyn

If we left this city behind
we might step out the side door
and into ragged trees, the whole woods
wild and skinny as a teenager. It's true
we might muscle around in dirt and log rot
for morels and wild onions, maybe make a salad
in a fallen nest, pick feathers
from our teeth. The girl's hair would snarl
into a yellow flame, we'd see her
mostly from behind and far away: a lit wick,
running. We might build a porch to hang
above some fat stream, for fun we'd jump
into the smudged middle, the place so deep
it's black. And even if it snowed for a month
without stopping I would never ever get tired
of walking in the midst of stricken air.
But we live here, in soot and slate and sometimes
thunder, and here is where my heart has
grown to shove the other organs aside, to
double-jump in syncopation with windows
up and down the block as they catch
and amplify the moving pulse of that stranger
driving through with his bass cranked high.
The ribs that keep me in don't quite keep
that muscled crashing still. Meaning: if you look
carefully, you can see it from the outside.
The day we leave is the day we start to live
forever in relation to the city's tune,
craning our necks from wherever we are
to see Brooklyn pink-ing up the sky like a flare.

Holly Anderson

4 Bovina Poems

1:

i. A hard green sheen
              burns
in the rear view
   as drunken spring gets sprung   and
         freshets of cloud
cascade the cleft
              of Route 28.

Is there time to slide
over Cambrian ledges
            of shattered,
    algaed shale
at Woodland Creek?
No, this doggie's nosing
                due west,
    gnawing the shank of the journey.
Hurrying home
          through blue stews
      of thunderstruck.

ii.   It's all right here
or very near
in its no-spangled splendor:

the chopper thrum of hummingbirds
     tapping bluestocking beebalm
    grass clots festering and roses rotting
above gnostic messages left
              in pewter colored
snail-scribbled texts
           under grizzled clouds
     pushing their blunt snouts   deep
into lavender rags of twilight
    as goldfinches punctuate
                    the green paragraphs

                    that lead to 7 pm.

2:

A crow's creaky caw
Pries me from sleep
And tears morning neat
Straight along its grain.

3:

This was the chapter
and
This was the verse:
A scourge of spurge
routed,
Torn out
by its white, hairy roots
Then,
Burdock banished
and malevolent Malva
yanked free
A woody taproot
as long as a forearm   revealed

4:

The goldenrod all crisped
and gone to dander.
The fairy fluff of milkweed.
Small fists of raddled apples
in a broken tree
rain down
on me.

The crows cry   "Ha! ha! HA!"

12.

Susie Berg

Love Is No Object

What we will give when love is no object.
Time. The foolishness of animal sounds.

One more story. A glass of water.
Endless pushes of the swing.

What others withheld.
Hair ribbons. Cupcakes. The word *love*.

We crave the chance to sugar the world,
repair the mistakes of ghosts.

January O'Neil

On the First Day of School

I return to a quiet house
and the empty hours
of autumn. I drink my cold,
black tea, listen to the dishwasher
trudge through its cycle, listen harder
for birdsong over a chain of split levels
and quarter-acre lots, a cacophony
of old habits reverberating like creaks
in the floorboards.
                              Then I rise
to bring the laundry from the basement
warm with impressions of little children,
tidy the kitchen, sweep the breakfast crumbs
from the counter into my cupped hand,
holding them like a sacred trust, I scatter them
over the trash can like a sacrifice, an offering.

Martha Silano

Said the Enemy to the Enemy,

all my life I've made mistakes,
all my life I've worn the headlamp

of lies, sent you places no map
could ever find—my detailed directions

knotted threads that take you
where worst-case cases arrive.

If I'm Atlas, forever holding up the sky,
you're the ground operation specialist,

tactically deployed; if I'm decided, you're
on the fence, the headless beast we call

the insurgent, sky-grabbing what feeds
our predator drones. We live together

on this Earth, each of us believing the other
a Grendel, while both of us govern benefits, costs;

that we'll never be friends goes without saying,
mainly because the hen will never lie down

with the horse, because a sandal is always a shoe
lacking sufficient support. Your government's short

on capacity, and so is mine (that's what we both call *central*).
In the land of Total Security: innumerable breaches,

throngs of reluctant followers; my Wet Ones, your rash,
and vice versa; my place in the sun, yours in the limelight.

Our mutual execution, our coalition, our taking turns
at toughest, most gristly, most flexed. All your life

you've made mistakes. All of my life I've wanted
what you want: grit, guts, valor, revenge. We're

a beautiful mess of potent force, of rage;
the problem is we both have what it takes.

Sadie Ducet

Really Seeing the Coffee Table

For all it took more than four months to arrive,
it does look good. He thinks the wood's too dark,
it doesn't match. But I prefer it. He tells how
he had to maintain the glass top's balance, level,
even as he matched and bolted corners
from underneath. *The directions must have assumed
zero gravity,* he jokes. But I'm not listening,

distracted by an article, or email, or the kids,
or even not distracted, just long married.

Later, drifting in or out of sleep,
I see him clearly, alone with the task he has
assigned himself, the awkward, slidey weight of it,
so hard to hold, hold up, and still fix all
in place. And how do we decipher these
instructions, always wordless, and the drill's
power cord just a bit too short?

Ana C. H. Silva

THE ORGAN OF CIRCULATION.

The heart is placed a little to the left

Fig. 23.

from all
parts of the body.
little tubes
carry

the heart to every
part of the body

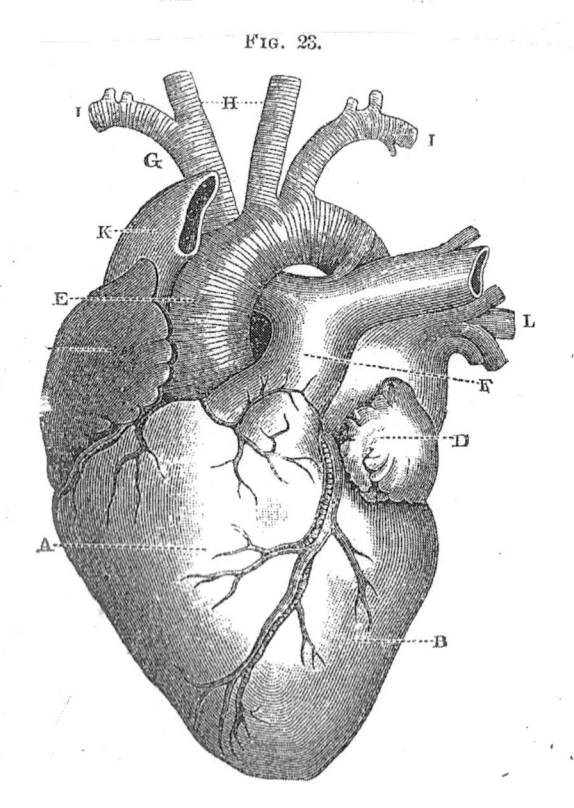

too small to be seen by the

exception to this rule

January O'Neil

What the Body Knows

The body knows it is part of a whole, its parts believed to be in good working order. It knows it's getting older, years ticking off like pages on a desk calendar, your doctor's appointment circled ink red. Try not to picture the body sitting alone in the waiting room. The body creaks up and down like a hardwood floor, you tell your doctor this; he says your breast is a snow globe. He says, Inside there's a snowstorm—my job is to decipher a bear from a moose in the snow. He flattens the breast with a low radiation sandwich press. The body wonders if its parts will turn into Brie cheese, if its fingers will fuse and become asparagus stalks. He says it's possible, but don't give it a second thought. He says insulate your body with spinach. He says true understanding of the body will enable it to live long and live well. But the body knows when its leg is being pulled. The body is a container of incidental materials. If it listens carefully, it can hear its own voice making the wrong sound.

Lesley Dame

The Answer

Even if it were a beacon, you'd be terrified.
I mean, come on, this sudden light flashes
in the starless sky and you're, what, *happy*?

You know that doesn't make sense. You know
that nothing is free; day and night each
have their own purpose. You are a moving
statue. You have no choice.

Now! says the light. *Not yet,* says the voice
inside your cold heart.

Fay Chiang

Reinvention

The fall comes

The daughter leaves for Spain
with her boyfriend;
they'll teach English and then
travel North Africa and the
Mediterranean---
happy and healthy and young
with great joy
my heart urges them: "Go!
See the world!"

Twenty years
surviving the breast cancer
I was so afraid
would not let me see
my little four year old girl
grow up and now only after
her graduation from college
do I realize
how long
I have held my breath

As the eldest I took care
of my father when he had colon cancer
my brother when he had Hodgkins disease
my mother when she had a cerebral aneurism
and their passing

I took care of my younger sister
when she had a heart attack and stroke---
nursing her back to recovery

So many of my friends with
HIV/AIDS and cancer
whose hands I held during
their last fading breaths---
honored and humbled

to witness
the gift and grace of
life ebbing into death---
cremations and burials,
memorial services;
their lives and friendships
etched in my heart

I think of the many young people at risk
I've nurtured these past four decades
hoping our time together
has put them on surer footing
in their journeys for happier
and fruitful lives---
and all that is possible

Community groups and
organizations where
we forced the issues of
representation and identity;
for social change and social justice
by creating art and culture
by and with those
whose voices had too
long been silenced----
silent no more

Yes, these were my first six decades and one.

II. Now
is a time for reinvention
even as the physical self is changing:
a heavy fatigue
failing eyesight
hearing dim from too many rock concerts
creaky joints and softening bone

III. Still
      the heart is strong and passionate
Still
      there is the need for purpose and to work for good
Still
      the need for laughter with friends and family young and old

   Still
         the need to love and be loved
   Still
         the need to dance and sing
   Still
         the need to write and paint
   Still
         the need to learn and grow
   Still
         the need to hike the highest peaks and let the spirit soar
   Still
         the need to change

Yes,
this is the time for reinvention
in the deep snows of winter;
let's see what comes in spring.

Marjorie Maddox

My Mother's Wedding Ends at Midnight

She wants to leave
or she doesn't, her new husband singing
love ballads at the Steinway with his children
and hers, his scratchy voice off-key but sweet
in its sentiment. She's half-listening,
alone at the door, measuring each guest's smile,
what else each might need. She's tired
in her happiness, but too polite to stop
the happiness of others gathered harmoniously
about the family piano. What else she hears
between false notes she keeps close to her own voice
that doesn't sing but follows closely
the words and where they will lead her.

Faith Williams

We are all each other's mothers

as we get older
we are all covering each other
with poems and teacakes and scarves.
Boots, we ask ? Are you
wearing your boots?
It's cold out there and
a lot of silence waits
out there.

Even the doctors
get immeasurably young
as we grow old. Are we
the oldest woman on earth?
Waking we climb through
the trap of stiff, sharp
bones to reach a cup
of coffee and painkiller pills.

As we get older we
become the scarves. We are
the warm hands, the note
in the lunchbox. As we grow
older, we reach out
our stubby, gnarled hands
and we do our best
to hold up the world.

Contributors' Notes

Elvis Alves works as a hospital chaplain. He is the author of the poetry collection *Bitter Melon*. Elvis lives in Brooklyn, NY. www.poemsbyelvis.blogspot.com

Holly Anderson is anthologized in *Up is Up, But So Is Down: New York's Downtown Literary Scene, 1974-1992* (NYU Press) *The Unbearables* & *The Unbearables Big Book of Sex* (Autonomedia) *First Person Intense* (Mudborn Press). 2014 in *'Wreckage of Reason 2'* (Spuyten Duyvil) *The Night She Slept With A Bear*, flash fictions and mesostics plus soundtrack by Chris Brokaw from Publication Studio, Portland OR., is also an iTunes app. www.smokemusic.tv/content/mission-burma-holly-anderson

E.J. Antonio is a 2009 fellow in Poetry from the New York Foundation for the Arts and a recipient of fellowships from the Hurston/Wright Foundation and the Cave Canem Foundation. She is the author of two chapbooks, *Every Child Knows*, Premier Poets Chapbook Series 2007, and *Solstice*, Red Glass Books, 2013. Her debut CD, *Rituals in the marrow: Recipe for a jam session* was released in the fall of 2010. www.ejantoniobluez.net

Priscilla Atkins' collection *The Cafe of Our Departure* is forthcoming from Sibling Rivalry Press. She teaches women's and gender studies at Hope College, in Holland, Michigan.

Felice Aull was in her 70s when her first chapbook, *The Music Behind Me*, was published in 2012. She is adjunct faculty in the Division of Medical Humanities in NYU's Department of Medicine and is on the editorial boards of *The Bellevue Literary Review* and *Literature and Medicine*. Her poems are published in *Front Porch Review, Hospital Drive, Third Wednesday, Ekphrasis, Poet Lore, Margie, The Healing Muse* and elsewhere. www.feliceaull.com

Rose Auslander is Poetry Editor of *Folded Word Press*, Editor of *unFold* magazine, co-editor of the Twitter anthology, *On A Narrow Windowsill*, and author of the chapbook *Folding Water*. Rose has read her poems on NPR; her poem "For You Mothers" received a Pushcart nomination and "Oh My" received a Best of the Net nomination. Also look for her work in *Sliver of Stone, Blue Fifth Review, Right Hand Pointing, Referential Magazine, The Dead Mule, My Favorite Bullet,* and the *Red Dirt Review*. And she blogs! http://roseauslander.wordpress.com

Mary Jo Balestreri has two books of poetry, *Joy in the Morning* and *gathering the harvest* published by Bellowing Ark Press, and a chapbook, *Best Brothers*, forthcoming from Tiger's Eye Press late spring, 2014. Mary Jo has three Pushcart nominations, and two Best of the Net. She is a founding member of Grace River Poets, an outreach for women's shelters, schools, and churches. maryjobalistreripoet.com

Kelly Bargabos, from Syracuse, NY, is the author of a memoir yet to be published. A graduate of the Creative Writing program of the Downtown Writer's Center, her work has appeared in previous volumes of *Mom Egg Review*, she has contributed articles to The Post-Standard and received Third Prize and Honorable Mention in the 2012 Soul-Making Keats Literary Competition. Kelly enjoys writing about the things that move her and hopes they move you too. www.kellybargabos.com

Poet/Visual Artist **Caroline Beasley-Baker's** poems have recently appeared online and in print in *La Fovea, MungBeing Magazine, Möbius/The Poetry Magazine, Mom Egg Review,* and *Qarrtsiluni*. She frequently uses words/poems in her visual work for which she has received a NYFA Fellowship in Painting and an NEA Grant in Collaborative Work. Her collection of poems, *For Lack Of Diamond Years,* was published in late 2013 by Pelekinesis Press (CA). www.carolinebeasley-baker.com (studio) and www.cbeasley-baker.com (book).

Patricia Behrens is a lawyer and writer who grew up in Massachusetts and now lives in Manhattan, on the Upper West Side. Her poetry previously has appeared in print and online, including in *The Main Street Rag* and *The Same*.

Andrea Beltran lives in El Paso, Texas, and moonlights as a poet and student. Her poems have recently appeared in *Superstition Review, Acentos Review, Blood Lotus,* and *caesura*. She blogs at andreakbeltran.wordpress.com.

Carol Berg's poems are forthcoming or in *The Journal, Spillway, Redactions, Pebble Lake Review, Fifth Wednesday Journal, Verse Wisconsin,* and in the anthologies *A Face To Meet The Faces: An Anthology of Contemporary Persona Poems* and *Bigger Than They Appear: An Anthology of Very Small Poems*. Her most recent chapbook, *Her Vena Amoris* (Red Bird Chapbooks), is available.

Susie Berg's first collection of poetry, *How to Get Over Yourself*, was published this fall by Piquant Press. She is also the author of The Starbucks Poetry Project (thestarbuckspoetryproject.blogspot.ca). Susie's work has appeared in several anthologies (*Desperately Seeking Susans; Seek It: Writers* and *Artists Do Sleep*) and periodicals (*carte blanche, In My Bed, Ars Medica*), and she is a frequent feature on Toronto's poetry stages. Follow her on twitter @SusieDBerg, or visit her online at sber40.wix.com/susieberg.

Genevieve Betts' work has appeared in (or is forthcoming from) *The Broadkill Review, A Narrow Fellow, Conversations Across Borders, The Bakery, Poetry Quarterly, NANO Fiction*, and other journals and anthologies. She received her MFA from Arizona State University and teaches poetry for Arcadia University's low-residency MFA program. She lives in Brooklyn with her husband and two sons.

Emily R. Blumenfeld's writing has appeared in both literary and scholarly publications, including *Mom Egg Review* and *The Journal of Poetry Therapy*. She is the author of two illustrated booklets, "Liquid Words" and "Love and Dust: Notes from the Kitchen Floor" (Prehensile Pencil Publications/The Feral Press).

Cheryl Boyce-Taylor is the founder of The Calypso Muse Reading Series. The author of three volumes of poetry, she is currently working on a memoir and a collection of poetry titled "The Red Bible".
A graduate of Stonecoast MFA poetry program, Cheryl's poems have been published in *ALOUD: Voices from the Nuyorican Poets Cafe, The Taos Journal of Arts and Culture, The Encyclopedia Project* and in *PLUCK! Journal of Affrilachian Arts & Culture*.

Deborah Brandon holds an MFA from the School of the Art Institute of Chicago. Her work appears or is forthcoming in *Bombay Gin, [PANK], Denver Quarterly, Moonshot, Cadillac Cicatrix, Hotel Amerika* and others. She lives in Tucson with her partner and two children.

Amy Brunvand is a librarian, part-time nature mystic and monthly contributor to *Catalyst* magazine in Salt Lake City, Utah. Her recent poetry has appeared in *Journal of Wild Culture, New Verse News, Elohi Gadugi Journal* and *Red Savina Review*. She is Mom to two kids, one of whom is currently experiencing the joys of puberty.

Following the advice of an accomplished writer who says, "You can get a lot done in 20 minutes," **Gabriella Burman** tries to find a few hours a week to devote to her craft, but more often finds herself allowing procrastination to take over, as when putting a chicken in the oven to feed her family. Writing well is arduous, but when the subject is her daughter, Michaela, it is an imperative Gabriella must heed.

Melisa "Misha" Cahnmann-Taylor is Professor of Language and Literacy Education and Program Chair of TESOL & World Language Education at the University of Georgia. She is a Fulbright Scholar in Oaxaca, Mexico writing a book about English speaking Americans moving South and becoming Spanish-English bilinguals. Winner of Dorothy Sargent Rosenberg Prizes, she has co-authored two books, *Teachers Act Up: Creating Multicultural Learning Communities Through Theatre* and *Arts-Based Research in Education,* numerous articles and poems http://teachersactup.com

Rosalie Calabrese is a native New Yorker and management consultant for the arts. In addition to press releases and poetry, she writes short stories and books and lyrics for musicals. Her work has appeared in magazines, journals, newspapers, anthologies, and on the Web. Among her credits are *Cosmopolitan, Poetry New Zealand, And Then, Möbius, Thema, Poetica, Jewish Currents, Phoenix, Mom Egg Review* and *The New York Times*. Her poems have also been set to music by several composers of art songs. She is listed in the Poets & Writers directory.

Nicole Callihan writes poems, stories and essays. Her work has appeared in *Painted Bride Quarterly, forklift, ohio, Cream City Review* and *Washington Square*. Co-author of the nonfiction book *Henry River Mill Village*, her first collection of poems, *Superloop*, is now available from Sock Monkey Press. A Senior Language Lecturer at New York University, Nicole lives in Brooklyn with her husband and daughters. Visit her website at www.nicolecallihan.com.

Fay Chiang is a poet and visual artist who believes culture is a spiritual and psychological weapon used for the empowerment of people and communities. Working at Project Reach (www.projectreach.org), a youth center for young people at risk in Chinatown/Lower East Side, she is also a member of Zero Capital, a collective of artists (www.zerocapital.net); the Orchard Street Advocacy and Wellness Center, which supports people affected by HIV/AIDS, cancer and other chronic illnesses. Battling her 8th bout of breast cancer, she is working on her memoir. *Seven Continents Nine Lives* (Bowery Books) is her most recent collection of poetry. And she is the mother of the inimitable Xian.

Vickie Cimprich's poetry collection, *Pretty Mother's Home – A Shakeress Daybook* (Broadstone Books, 2007) was researched at the Shaker Village of Pleasant Hill, Kentucky with the support of two grants from the Kentucky Foundation For Women. http://www.broadstonebooks.com/Vickie_Cimprich_Page.html Her work also appears in appears in *The Journal of Kentucky Studies, The African American Review, Plainsongs* and *Bigger Than They Appear: Anthology of Very Short Poems* (Accents Press, 2011).

Patrice Boyer Claeys lives in Chicago and attends Alice George's Serious Play Poetry Workshop. She is a graduate of the University of Chicago's Writer's Studio. Her work has appeared in *Mom Egg Review, The Found Poetry Journal* and *ARDOR*, as well as *The Journal* of Northwestern University and the *Poet and Artist Chapbook* of the Northwest Cultural Council, where she leads the occasional workshop.

Marion Deutsche Cohen's new memoir, *Still the End: Memoir of a Nursing Home Wife*, was just released by Unlimited Publishers (IA). This is the sequel to her memoir, *Dirty Details: The Days and Nights of a Well Spouse* (Temple University Press). Her books total 21, and her children/grands total 8. She teaches math and writing at Arcadia University in Glenside, PA, and is the author of "Crossing the Equal Sign", a poetry book about the experience of math.

Lesley Dame is co-founder of and poetry and nonfiction editor for *damselfly press*. She is author of the chapbook, *Letting Out the Ghosts*, and her poems, reviews, and stories have also appeared in many online and print journals. Dame happily lives, writes, and edits in some rural town somewhere. www.wix.com/lesleydame/poet.

Jacqueline Doyle lives in the San Francisco Bay Area. She has published creative nonfiction in *South Dakota Review, Frontiers, Southern Indiana Review,* and *Ninth Letter* online, and flash nonfiction in *Sweet, elimae, Bluestem,* and *Prime Number*. She was recently nominated for a Pushcart Prize by *South Loop Review*, and has a "Notable Essay" listed in Best American Essays 2013. This is her second appearance in *Mom Egg Review*. www.facebook.com/authorjacquelinedoyle.

Sadie Ducet's poetry appears in such places as *Rose Red Review, The Progressive,* and *Midwestern Gothic*. Her work is curated by Sarah Busse, co-editor of *Verse Wisconsin* and Cowfeather Press, and one of Madison, Wisconsin's Poets Laureate. www.cowfeatherpress.org

Pat Falk teaches writing and literature at Nassau Community College in Garden City, NY. The author of four books of poetry and prose, her work has appeared in *The New York Times Book Review, Thirteenth Moon,* and *The Mickle Street Review, Women Artists News* and *The American Book Review*. www.patfalk.net

Kate Falvey's work has appeared in numerous print and online journals, including the *Yellow Medicine Review, The Stony Thursday Book,* and previous issues of *Mom Egg Review*. She has two chapbooks out, *What the Sea Washes Up* (Dancing Girl Press) and *Morning Constitutional with Sunhat and Bolero* (Green Fuse Poetic Arts). She edits the *2 Bridges Review*, published through City Tech of the City University of New York, where she teaches, and is on the editorial board of the *Bellevue Literary Review*.

Sandra L. Faulkner is director of Women's, Gender and Sexuality Studies at Bowling Green State University. Her poetry appears in places like *Women & Language, Storm Cellar, Literary Mama,* and *Sugar House Review*. She authored two chapbooks, *Hello Kitty Goes to College* (dancing girl press) *and K4, M1: Knit Four, Make One* (forthcoming Kattywompus). Her poetry memoir is forthcoming from Sense Publishers. She lives in NW Ohio with her partner, their warrior girl, and a rescue mutt.

Jessica Feder-Birnbaum is a writer and theatre arts professional whose passion is building community through theatre. She has written and directed plays for New York theatres, dance companies, schools, and synagogues.

Her articles have appeared in both print and on-line media. She writes content for educational video and business websites. She is a New York State Council on the Arts MFTA summer institute scholarship recipient. She is grateful for the Mom Egg community.

Chelsea Lemon Fetzer is a poet and fiction writer. She holds an MFA in Creative Writing from Syracuse University. Her work has appeared in literary journals such as *Stone Canoe, Callaloo, Tin House*, and the *Mississippi Review*. It can also be found online at *Poets for Living Waters,* and *Sugar Mule*. She founded The Create Collective, Inc. and additionally leads writing workshops across New York City in collaboration with PEN American Center's Reading and Writing Program, The New York Writer's Coalition, and independently.

Stephanie Feuer's articles and essays have appeared in *The New York Times, The New York Press*, on *bettyconfidential.com*, previous issues of *Mom Egg Review* and in numerous anthologies and literary magazines. In June, 2014, Hipso Media will publish her debut young adult novel, *Drawing Amanda*. Read more on stephaniefeuer.com and follow her on twitter @StephanieFeuer.

Jamie Asaye FitzGerald's poetry has appeared in *Works & Days, Cultural Weekly* and *Literary Mama* among other journals and anthologies, as well as on public buses. She received an MFA in poetry from San Diego State University and an Academy of American Poets College Prize at the University of Southern California. Originally from Hawaii, she lives in Los Angeles with her husband and daughter, and works for Poets & Writers. She is expecting another daughter in June. http://alunir.blogspot.com/

Laura Davies Foley is the author of three poetry collections. Her latest, *The Glass Tree*, won a Foreword Book of the Year Award, and was a Finalist for the New Hampshire Writer's Project, Outstanding Book of Poetry. She's the mother of three grown children, the youngest of whom now lives at the wonderful Plowshare Farm in Greenfield NH. www.lauradaviesfoley.com

Susan Fox's poems have appeared in journals ranging from *Poetry* and *The Paris Review* and *Boulevard* to *The New York Times*. She was born in Ohio, taught in New York, and has lived in Rome, Paris, and rural France. An opera to her libretto set in World War II was performed in New York, and her screenplay of another Holocaust story was optioned for film. She lives in Manhattan with her husband, physicist Stephen Orenstein.

Lisha Garcia is the author of *Blood Rivers*, her initial full-length poetry collection published by Blue Light Press and *This Stone Will Speak* from Pudding House. She has an MFA from Vermont College of Fine Arts and currently resides in San Antonio, Texas with her beloved four-legged children. Her second poetry collection, *A Rope of Luna* is forthcoming. She is the mother of two children now in their 20's. www.lishagarcia.com.

Elisa A. Garza has published two chapbooks, *Entre la Claridad* (Mouthfeel Press) and *Familia* (a bestseller for The Portlandia Group). Her poems have been awarded a Literature Fellowship from the Texas Commission on the Arts and the Emerging Writer Award from the Alfredo Cisneros del Moral Foundation. She has taught writing, literature, and Women's Studies courses in the community and at the university level. Elisa blogs about Catholic mothering, healthy eating, and writing at www.tercets.blogspot.com.

Nancy Gerber is an advanced clinical candidate at the Academy of Clinical and Applied Psychoanalysis in Livingston, New Jersey. Her third book, *Fire and Ice,* is forthcoming from Arseya. She is grateful to her 92-year-old mother-in-law, Evelyn Gerber, for reminding her to live each day to the fullest, "because you never know what the next day will bring."

Heather Haldeman lives in Pasadena, California. She has been married to her husband, Hank, for thirty-five years and has three grown children. Her work has been published in *The Christian Science Monitor, Chicken Soup for the Soul, From Freckles to Wrinkles, Grandmother Earth, Mom Egg Review* and numerous online journals. She has received first, second and third prizes for her essays.

Elaine Handley is Professor of Writing and Literature at SUNY Empire State College. She has published poetry and fiction in a variety of magazines and anthologies. Handley's most recent chapbook of poetry is *Letters to My Migraine* and she is completing a novel, *Deep River*, about the Underground Railroad in Upstate New York.

Jane Harrington has written four books for children and young adults (Scholastic, Lerner), and she is now crafting adult fiction and creative nonfiction in Virginia's Shenandoah Valley, where she lives, writes and teaches college writing. Her work has been or will soon be published in *Irish America* magazine, *Ten: Carlow University's MFA Anniversary Anthology,* and the *Chautauqua* literary journal. Jane has been awarded a 2014 fellowship from the Virginia Center for Creative Arts.

Lois Marie Harrod's 13th and 14th poetry collections appeared in 2013: *Fragments from the Biography of Nemesis* (Word Tech: Cherry Grove) and *How Marlene Mae Longs for Truth* (Dancing Girl Press). Over 500 of her poems have appeared in literary journals and online ezines from *American Poetry Review* to *Zone 3* and including *The Colorado Review*. She teaches Creative Writing at The College of New Jersey. http://loismarieharrod.org/home.html

Amy Lee Heinlen is currently working towards a MFA in poetry and publishing from Chatham University. Her poems have appeared in *Voices in the Attic*, volumes 18 and 19, and the *Red Clay Review*. She works as a librarian in Pittsburgh, Pennsylvania, where she lives with her husband, their recently-arrived daughter, and two cats.

Claudia D. Hernández was born and raised in Guatemala. She's a photographer, poet, translator, and a bilingual educator residing in Los Angeles. Claudia is currently pursuing an MFA in Creative Writing for Young People, with an emphasis in poetry, at Antioch University, Los Angeles. Various online literary journals and anthologies throughout the United States, the UK, Canada, Mexico, and Spain have published her work. She is the founder of the ongoing project: Today's Revolutionary Women of Color. www.todaysrevolutionarywomenofcolor.com

Matt Hohner holds an M.F.A. in Writing and Poetics from Naropa University in Boulder, Colorado. His work has appeared or is forthcoming in *The Baltimore Review, Dancing Shadow Review, September Eleven: Maryland Voices, Poets Against the War* (online), *The Potomac* (online), *Lily* (online), and other publications. Hohner teaches high school English in Baltimore, Maryland, where he lives with his wife, Jen, and his cat, Maxie, and enjoys kayaking on the Chesapeake Bay, mountain biking, and hiking.

Louisa Howerow's latest poems appeared in *Naugatuck River Review, Arc Poetry Magazine (Canada),* and *Antiphon*. She's pleased to once more be part of *Mom Egg Review*.

Electra Hunzeker is an MFA student in fiction at New Mexico State University. Her fiction and non-fiction has been published in various magazines, including *Misfit Magazine* and *Minnesota Parent*. She's also a mother and a college composition instructor.

Vicki Iorio is a native Long Islander and a graduate of Hofstra University. *Poems from the Dirty Couch* is Iorio's first published poetry collection.

Elizabeth Johnston is a founding member of the Straw Mat Writer's Circle in Rochester, NY where she also teaches writing, literature, and gender studies at Monroe Community College. When she is not teaching, grading, helping her daughters with their homework, working as a literacy volunteer, facilitating writing workshops at the Breast Cancer Coalition, etc, etc, she finds solace in poetry…and sleep.

Hester Jones is a British Artist based in London UK. Her work is an ongoing investigation into culturally constructed, gendered identities; she is interested in the performative and participatory qualities of photography. www.hesterjones.com

Donna Katzin is executive director of Shared Interest, a not-for-profit investment fund that provides access to credit and technical support in Southern Africa – particularly to women of color – and works to break down barriers between banks and low-income communities. A former labor organizer and anti-apartheid activist, she is the author of a book of poems about the new South Africa entitled *With These Hands*, and the proud mother of Sari and Daniel Altschuler.

Caledonia Kearns is the editor of *Cabbage and Bones* and *Motherland,* two anthologies of writing by Irish American women. She holds an MFA in poetry from Hunter College and lives in Brooklyn with a lovely and amazing teenager and writes poems and occasional essays about television.

Kate Kostelnik earned her Ph.D. in English from the University of Nebraska, Lincoln. She currently works at Washington College. Her fiction, which earned a 2007 NJ State Arts Council Fellowship, has appeared in *Hayden's Ferry* and *Fifth Wednesday* among others. Her scholarship has been published in *Creative Writing Teaching: Theory and Practice, A Guide to Creative Writing Pedagogies,* and is forthcoming in *Pedagogy*. This is her first published poem.

Kathryn Kysar is the author of two books of poetry, *Dark Lake* and *Pretend the World*, and editor of *Riding Shotgun: Women Write About Their Mothers*. She has received fellowships and residencies from the Minnesota State Arts Board, the National Endowment for the Humanities, and the Anderson Center for Interdisciplinary Studies. She chairs the creative writing program at Anoka-Ramsey Community College. Her website is www.kathrynkysar.com, and she lives with her family in Saint Paul.

Ashleigh Lambert is the author of the chapbook *Ambivalent Amphibians* (Dancing Girl Press). Her poetry and other writing has been published in *Anti-, Bone Bouquet, Coldfront, Elimae, McSweeney's Internet Tendency, Redivider, The Rumpus,* and *Sink Review*. She currently lives in New York City with her spouse and daughter, and online at ashleigh-lambert.tumblr.com.

Most recently, poems by **Elizabeth Lara** have appeared in *Mom Egg Review, Edna, Confluencia in the Valley: The First Five Years of Converging with Words,* and *The Vine Leaves Literary Journal*. In 2011 she was a resident at the Millay Colony in Austerlitz, NY. She writes with the Hot Poets Collective, whose anthology, *Of Fire, Of Iron*, was published in 2012. She lives in New York and Santo Domingo, Dominican Republic.

Issa M. Lewis is a graduate of New England College's MFA in Poetry program and currently teaches composition at Davenport University. Her poems have previously appeared in *Backbone Press, Looseleaf Tea, Extract(s), Scapegoat Review, Pearl, Naugatuck River Review,* and *Switched-On Gutenberg*. She lives in West Michigan.

Tsaurah Litzky's *Flasher - a Memoir*, just published by Audible Books, is also available on Amazon as an E-book for Kindle. Her most recent poetry collection, *Cleaning The Duck*, was published by Bowery Books. Tsaurah is very proud to have her poem included in *Mom Egg Review* because it rocks so steady warm and strong, it makes her think of her mothers arms.

Diane Lockward is the author of *The Crafty Poet: A Portable Workshop* (Wind Publications, 2013) and three poetry books, most recently *Temptation by Water*. Her previous books are *What Feeds Us*, which received the 2006 Quentin R. Howard Poetry Prize, and *Eve's Red Dress*. Her poems have been included in such journals as *Harvard Review, Spoon River Poetry Review,* and *Prairie Schooner*. Her work has also been featured on *Poetry Daily, Verse Daily,* and *The Writer's Almanac*.

Director of Creative Writing and Professor of English at Lock Haven University, **Marjorie Maddox** has published nine books of poetry, most recently *Local News from Someplace Else* and a 2013 ebook of *Perpendicular As I* (1994 Sandstone Book Award). Co-editor of *Common Wealth: Contemporary Poets on Pennsylvania* and two children's books, *A Crossing of Zebras: Animal Packs in Poetry* and *Rules of the Game: Baseball Poems*, she lives with her husband and two children in PA. www.marjoriemadox.com

Charlotte Mandel has published eight books of poetry, the most recent, *Life Work*, from David Robert Books. Previous titles include two poem-novellas of feminist biblical revision. Awards include winner of the 2012 New Jersey Poets Prize. She edited the Eileen W. Barnes Award Anthology, *Saturday's Women*. She has published a series of articles on the role of cinema in the life and work of poet H.D. Visit her at www.charlottemandel.com

Jennifer Martelli was born and raised in Massachusetts, and graduated from Boston University and The Warren Wilson M.F.A. Program for Writers (M.F.A.). She's taught high school English as well as women's literature at Emerson College in Boston. Her work has appeared, or will appear, *The Denver Quarterly, Folio, Calliope, Kalliope, The Mississippi Review, The Bellingham Review, Kindred, Bitterzoet, ZigZag Folio, The Inflectionist Review, Sugared Water, Slippery Elm, Tar River Review* and *Bop Dead City*. She was a finalist for the Sue Elkind Poetry Prize and a recipient of the Massachusetts Cultural Council Grant in Poetry. Her chapbook, *Apostrophe*, was published in 2011 by Big-Table Publishing Company. Right now, she is at home with her two kids, involved in the poetry scene in Salem, Massachusetts, and teaching occasional classes at the Peabody Library.

Libby Maxey has a Masters degree in Medieval Studies from Cornell University and has worked as an archival assistant, an elementary school paraprofessional, a voice teacher, a classical singer and a freelance editor. She is on the editorial board of the online journal *Literary Mama*, which has also published her poetry. She is a founding member of the acquisitions editorial board of Thornapple Books, a small press imprint for literary fiction.

John Minczeski's most recent poetry collection, *A Letter to Serafin*, was published by the University of Akron Press in 2009. His poems have appeared in *Agni, Big City Lit, Mid-American Review*, and elsewhere. He lives in St. Paul, Minnesota.

Katrinka Moore's latest poetry book, *Numa*, is being published by Aqueduct Press in 2014. She is the author of *Thief* and *This is Not a Story*, which won the Finishing Line Press New Women's Voices prize. Recent work appears online in *MungBeing, Otoliths, Dépositions, le Blog*, and *First Literary Review-East*.

Samina Najmi is associate professor of English at California State University, Fresno. A scholar of race, gender, and war in American literature, she discovered the rewards of more personal kinds of writing in a 2011 CSU Summer Arts course. Her creative nonfiction has appeared or is forthcoming in *The Progressive, Pilgrimage, The Rumpus, Gargoyle, Chautauqua*, and other publications. Her essay "Abdul" won *Map Literary's* 2012 nonfiction prize. Samina grew up in Pakistan and England, and now lives with her family in California's San Joaquin Valley.

Lesléa Newman is the author of 65 books for readers of all ages including the poetry collections *Still Life With Buddy, Nobody's Mother,* and *October Mourning: A Song For Matthew Shepard*. "In The ICU" is taken from *I Carry My Mother*, a recently completed poetry collection about a daughter's journey through her mother's illness and death. A former Poet Laureate of Northampton, MA, Lesléa Newman teaches at Spalding University's Brief-Residency MFA In Writing Program. www.lesleanewman.com

January Gill O'Neil is the author of *Underlife* (CavanKerry Press, December 2009), and a forthcoming collection, *Misery Islands* (CavanKerry Press, fall 2014). She is the executive director of the Massachusetts Poetry Festival and an assistant professor of English at Salem State University. She lives with her two children in Beverly, MA.

Erin Fillmore Olds has always loved telling stories, but it wasn't until third grade that she began to write them down. A teacher complimented an assignment and that was all it took. Olds cut her teeth on Nancy Drew-like fiction, but quickly expanded. Poetry, essays, YA novels, and adult novels are all equal game. When she isn't writing, she is taking photographs, playing with her dogs, or spending time with her sweet husband and son.

Eve Packer: Bronx-born, poet/performer, has appeared widely, solo, w/music, in theatre and dance. She has received grants from NYSCA, NYFA, the NEH, Puffin Foundations, and awards from *Time to Consider: the Arts Respond to 9/11,* also from the Chester H. Jones Foundation, *Downtown* and *Conceit* Magazines. She has published three poetry books: *skulls head samba, playland poems 1994-2004,* and *new nails(*2011) (Fly By Night), and has 4 full poetry/jazz CD's, and *first and last* w/saxophonist Noah Howard; in 2013 she released *my champagne waltz* w/ pianist/vocalist Stephanie Stone & multi-instrumentalist Daniel Carter. Lives downtown and swims daily.

P. A. Pashibin is a poet and folk artist who earned her MFA at Hamline University's College of Liberal Arts. She is presently working on a collection of multi-generational mother/daughter poems; a series of picasiette mosaic "pages" that incorporate and are inspired by her individual poems; a picture book that she is writing in collaboration with the visual artist, Roseann Mammoser; and a cookbook.
http://www.mnartists.org/artistHome.do?rid=166412

Theta Pavis is a poet, award-winning journalist and blogger whose work has appeared in everything from *The Journal of New Jersey Poets* to *New York Family* magazine. An expert in nonprofit communications, she has worked for numerous women's agencies, including the Center for Global Women's Leadership. She serves as the Media Adviser to *The Gothic Times*, a student newspaper published at New Jersey City University, where she also teaches.

Jayne A. Pierce is an award-winning librarian, feminist, activist, writer and disabled mother. She has published widely in various formats. Currently a resident of Woodbridge, New Jersey, Pierce is a New York City citizen at heart.

Andrea Potos is the author of four poetry collections, including *We Lit the Lamps Ourselves* (Salmon Poetry, Ireland) and *Yaya's Cloth* (Iris Press). Another collection is forthcoming in 2015. Her poems can be found widely online and in print. She lives in Madison, Wisconsin with her family.

Kyle Potvin's poetry has appeared in *The New York Times, Measure, The Huffington Post, JAMA, Blue Unicorn, Alimentum,* and on *BBC's World Update,* among others. She was named a finalist for the 2008 Howard Nemerov Sonnet Award. Her first poetry collection, *Sound Travels on Water,* was published in November 2012 by Finishing Line Press.

Marcia J. Pradzinski is a poet and memoirist living in Skokie, Illinois. Her poetry has appeared in a number of journals including *Rhino, After Hours, Avocet, JOMP, Blue Hour Magazine, Exact Change Press* and several anthologies. Her work has won awards in the Jo-Anne Hirshfield Memorial Contest and other competitions. She is currently working on a collection of poetry. Writing, especially poetry, helps her stay sane in her otherwise chaotic life.

Kristin Procter is a motherwriter who currently lives in Massachusetts, was born Canadian, partnered with a Brit, and birthed Australian babies. She enjoys yoga, knitting and entering into conversations best avoided in polite company. Kristin has never been mistaken for polite company. Her work was included in *First time Mum: A collection of experiences of becoming a mum for the first time.*

Kristin Roedell is the author of *Seeing in the Dark* (Tomato Can Press), *and Girls with Gardenias,* (Flutter Press). Her work has been published in *The Journal of the American Medical Association, Switched on Gutenberg, and CHEST.* She is a Pushcart Prize and Best of the Web nominee, winner of *NISA's 11th Annual Open Minds Quarterly Poetry Contest,* and a finalist in the 2103 *Crab Creek Review* poetry contest. http://cicadas-sing.ucoz.com/

Erika Bailey Rybczyk-- I find the first thing I do is define myself as a mother, which is certainly appropriate here. I have three children, and two "bonus children," all whom are a constant source of laughs, surprises and stress. Writing is my greatest joy and the thing that keeps me sane. My dream is to have a tiny little cottage filled with windows and books and a big old desk that is just for me.

Gerard Sarnat authored two poetry collections, 2010's *HOMELESS CHRONICLES from Abraham to Burning Man* and 2012's *Disputes*. His pieces appeared/are forthcoming in over eighty journals/anthologies. Harvard/Stanford educated, Gerry's a physician who's set up and staffed clinics for the disenfranchised, a CEO of health care organizations, and a Stanford professor. For The Huffington Post's review, etc.; visit GerardSarnat.com. "Lap" will appear in his third collection, "17s," in which each poem, stanza, or line has seventeen syllables.

Martha Silano is the author of four books of poetry, including *The Little Office of the Immaculate Conception,* chosen by Campbell McGrath as the winner of the 2010 Saturnalia Books Poetry Prize, and *Reckless Lovely* (Saturnalia 2014). She is also co-editor, with Kelli Russell Agodon, of *The Daily Poet: Day-By-Day Prompts For Your Writing Practice* (Two Sylvias Press 2013). Martha serves as poetry editor of *Crab Creek Review* and teaches at Bellevue College. Her blog is Blue Positive, http://bluepositive.blogspot.com

Robin Silbergleid is the author of the chapbooks *Pas de Deux: Prose and Other Poems* (Basilisk Press, 2006) and *Frida Kahlo, My Sister* (Finishing Line Press, 2014), as well as the forthcoming memoir *Texas Girl* (Demeter Press). Her essays and poems have appeared recently in *Hospital Drive, The Citron Review, Thin Air, Rattle,* and elsewhere. She lives in East Lansing, Michigan, where she directs the Creative Writing Program at Michigan State University, and raises her two children.

Ana C. H. Silva lives in Spanish Harlem, NYC with her husband and twin daughters. Her poetry has been published in *Podium, Mom Egg Review, the nth position, Snow Monkey* and *Anemone Sidecar*. She won the 2010 inaugural Rachel Wetzsteon Memorial Poetry Prize at the 92ndSt. Y Unterberg Poetry Center.

Ellen McGrath Smith teaches at the University of Pittsburgh. Poems have appeared in *Cimarron, Bayou, Quiddity, Sententia, The American Poetry Review,* and others. Her work has been recognized with an AROHO Orlando Prize, an Academy of American Poets award, a Rainmaker Award from *Zone 3* magazine, and a 2007 Individual Artist grant from the Pennsylvania Council on the Arts. A chapbook of her poems, *Scatter, Feed,* will be published this year by Seven Kitchens Press.

Shanalee Smith was born and raised in Tucson, Arizona. Her poetry has appeared in or is forthcoming from *Sandscript, Slipstream, Neon* and *Thin Air*. She is mother of two monsters, Tristan the Fashionista and Oliver the Indestructible. Shanalee is also the notorious ringleader of the Shameless Word-Artist Society, a collective of poets intent on gaining dominion over the universe using spoons and phosphorescence.

John Warner Smith's poems have appeared in *Ploughshares, Callaloo, The Worcester Review, Bloodroot, Pembroke, Pluck!, Fourteen Hills, American Athenaeum, Quiddity* and other literary journals. His book-length manuscript was a finalist in the 2013 Crab Orchard Series in Poetry First Book Award competition, and his short collection, "Hunting Dragonflies," was a finalist in the 2012 Poetry Contest of the Tennessee Williams / New Orleans Literary Festival. John resides in Baton Rouge, where he teaches English and Creative Writing at Southern University. A Cave Canem Fellow, he earned his MFA at the University of New Orleans.

Golda Solomon is Poet-In-Residence at Blue Door Gallery, Yonkers, NY, as well as professor, mom and grandmother. *Medicine Woman of Jazz*, her latest collection, (World Audience Publishers, 2012) is available on amazon.com and barnesandnoble.com. Golda performs her words with a roster of fine musicians and is most excited about the birth of her latest project, Jazz and Poetry Choir Collective, conducted by Michael T.A. Thompson. www.jazzjaunts.com

Cassie Premo Steele's poetry has been nominated three times for a Pushcart Prize. She is the author of 13 books; her most recent is called *13* and includes poems in the voice of a divorced mother and her 13-year-old daughter. Her website is www.cassiepremosteele.com

Lisa A. Sturm coauthored the book *From the Wise Women of Israel: Folklore and Memoirs* with Doris B. Gold (Biblio Press, 1993). She recently completed her first novel, *Life on the Other Side*, which was born out of her experiences as an inner-city psychotherapist. Her short stories and creative nonfiction have been published or are forthcoming in *Moment Magazine, Willow Review, The New Jersey Jewish News, Serving House Journal,* and *The Jewish Standard*.

Judy Swann is a poet and bicycle commuter, whose work has been published in many venues both in print and online. She lives in a tiny yellow house in Ithaca, NY.

Melanie Sweeney holds an MFA from New Mexico State University, and her recent work has appeared in *Foundling Review, Reunion: The Dallas Review,* and *Rougarou*. She lives in Spring, Texas, with her husband, son, and dog.

Christine Swint's poems appear recently or are forthcoming in *Slant, a Journal of Poetry, Tampa Review, Birmingham Poetry Review,* and others. Her poems have been nominated for the Pushcart Prize, Best of the Net, and Best New Poets. She lives in metro Atlanta, Georgia with her husband, two sons, and her dogs, Red and Duffy. For samples of Christine's writing, visit her blog, Balanced on the Edge, at http://christineswint.com

Abigail Templeton-Greene's poetry has been published in *McSweeneys, RATTLE, Pilgrimage, The Tulane Review,* and several other journals. She has an MFA from Antioch University Los Angeles and is a winner of the 2011 Lighthouse Writers Seven Deadly Sins Writing Contest. She was also recently nominated for the Friends of the University of the Sciences Pennsylvania Writing Award. Abigail teaches Creative Writing at Florence Crittenton High School in Denver, Colorado.

Geeta Tewari is a poet living in New York City. Her work has been published in *Ibbetson Street Magazine* and *Podium Magazine*.

Becky Tipper's short fiction and non-fiction has appeared in *Literary Mama, Mom Egg Review, The Bridport Prize Anthology,* and *Scraps: the National Flash Fiction Day anthology 2013*. She currently lives in Texas but will soon be relocating to Maine with her husband and two children. You can find her at: thebookflea.com

Meredith Trede's book, *Field Theory*, was published by SFA Press(2011). A Toadlily Press founder, her chapbook, *Out of the Book*, was in the inaugural Quartet Series. Other journals that have published her work include *Barrow Street, The Cortland Review, Gargoyle,* and *The Paris Review*. She has been awarded residency fellowships at Blue Mountain Center, Ragdale, Saltonstall, The Virginia Center for the Creative Arts, and the 2012 Nicholson Political Poetry Award. www.meredithtrede.com

Claudia Van Gerven teaches writing in Boulder, Colorado. Her poems have been published in a number journals, including *Prairie Schooner, Comstock Review* and *Calyx*, as well as numerous anthologies. Her work has been nominated for the Pushcart Prize. Her chapbook, *The Ends of Sunbonnet Sue*, won the Angel Fish Press Poetry Prize, and her most recent chapbook is *Amazing Grace* (Green Fuse Poetic Arts, 2010).

Wendy Vardaman (wendyvardaman.com) is the author of *Obstructed View* (Fireweed Press), co-editor of *Echolocations, Poets Map Madison*, co-editor/webmaster of *Verse Wisconsin* (versewisconsin.org), and co-founder/co-editor of Cowfeather Press (cowfeatherpress.org). She is one of Madison, Wisconsin's two Poets Laureate (2012-2015). Twitter: @wendylvardaman. Tumblr blog: live art(s) art live(s).

Cindy Veach's poetry has appeared in *Chelsea, Prairie Schooner, Chicago Review, Carolina Quarterly, Poet Lore, Sou'wester* and others and work is forthcoming in *Paterson Literary Review, Connotation Press, Stoneboat* and *Crab Creek Review*. She was a finalist for the Ann Stanford Prize, and the recipient of an honorable mention in the Ratner-Ferber-Poet Lore Prize and the Crab Creek Review Poetry Prize. She lives in Manchester, Massachusetts.

Eti Wade is an artist and academic. Her art practice is a personal investigation of the limits of maternal subjectivity expressed through photography and video and she also writes on the subject of the maternal gaze in contemporary photographic art. Eti is a lecturer teaching at the University of West London, she is the mother of three boys aged 20, 13 and 4 and lives in London, England.

Nicola Waldron, a native of the United Kingdom, writes poetry and non-fiction from her home in South Carolina, where she teaches creative writing and tries to keep up with a son and daughter. Other recent work can be found in *Agni, The Common Free State Review,* and *Her Kind*.

Originally from Louisiana, **Anna Lowe Weber** currently lives in Huntsville, Alabama, where she teaches creative writing and composition at the University of Alabama in Huntsville. Her work has appeared or is forthcoming in *The Florida Review, Iowa Review, Rattle,* and *Ninth Letter*, among others.

Arlene Weiss spent 15 years working for major ad agencies. She also free-lanced for Manischevitz Wines (radio commercials on the air) and created successful direct mail packages for R. R. Donnelly, Amoco Motor Club and Grandview Palos Verdes.

Zoë Ryder White lives in Brooklyn with her husband and daughter. Her poems have appeared in *Threepenny Review, Painted Bride Quarterly, Subtropics,* and *Crab Creek Review*.

Faith Williams, mother of 5 children, was most recently a children's librarian in a DC charter school, and for a long time taught English, mostly part time and mostly to freshmen. She has published poems in *Poet Lore, Nimrod, Primavera,* and *Calyx,* among others.

Seretha D. Williams is an English professor at Georgia Regents University in Augusta, Georgia, and a mother of three children. She is the co-editor of *Afterimages of Slavery*, a critical anthology, and the author of "'Waiting for the Spider to Come Home': Mothers and Mothering in *Lalita Tademy's Cane River*", a chapter in *Reclaiming Home, Remembering Motherhood, Rewriting History: African American and Afro-Caribbean Women's Literature in the Twentieth Century*.

Carolyn Williams-Noren makes a living as a communications coordinator for an affordable housing non-profit. She received a 2013 Artist Initiative grant from the Minnesota State Arts Board, and is the founder and caretaker of a free poetry library (littlepoetrylibrary.org) in her Minneapolis neighborhood. www.williams-noren.com.

Laura Madeline Wiseman is the author of twelve collections of poetry, including *Queen of the Platform* (Anaphora Literary Press, 2013). She is the editor of *Women Write Resistance: Poets Resist Gender Violence* (Hyacinth Girl Press, 2013). Her work has appeared in *Prairie Schooner, Margie,* and *Feminist Studies*. She has received an Academy of American Poets Award, a Prairie Schooner Award, and the Wurlitzer Foundation Fellowship. She has a doctorate from the University of Nebraska-Lincoln. www.lauramadelinewiseman.com

Emily Wolahan's first book, *HINGE,* is forthcoming in April 2014. Her work has appeared in *Boston Review, DIAGRAM, Drunken Boat, the National Poetry Review, elimae* and *New Linear Perspectives*. She lives in San Francisco and co-edits *JERRY* Magazine.

Margaret Young is the author of two collections, *Willow From the Willow* and *Almond Town,* and is currently working on translations of contemporary Argentine poetry. She lives in Beverly Massachusetts and teaches at Endicott College.

About Hester Jones' A SHOW OF HANDS (p. 91-92)

Hester Jones realized "A Show of Hands" during an artist residency in a London care home with over 30 people living with dementia, many of whom were mothers. The artist collated the life stories behind each pair of hands to create a book and exhibition. For more photographs and information about this project, please visit her website, www.hesterjones.com.

Eti Wade on MIGRANT MOTHERS (Cover and pp. 61-63)

'Migrant Mothers' is a series of photographs of mothers with their children. The title is a homage to Dorothea Lange's famous photograph 'Migrant Mother' which recorded a young mother, aged before her time, holding three young children close to her body, her face showing the hardship she suffers through caring for her children while struggling with extreme poverty.

My mothers are migrants, they are economic migrants who have left their home countries to work in rich, Western economies. To be able to gain entry and work long hours the mothers have to leave their children behind to be cared for by grandparents or other family members. They often leave their children at a very young age, sometimes even a few months old. Thanks to Skype and other internet communication channels they get to see them (visually) regularly. What they do not get to do as mothers is be with their children, physically. They cannot hug, comfort, change nappies, clean, kiss, kiss better or simply share a physical space for months and sometimes for years.

My Migrant Mothers are photographed together with their children. Both mother and child are present at the sitting, only one (mother) is in London, UK, sharing a physical space with me in her apartment and the other (child) is in the Philippines, sitting in front of their computer as they do regularly to be with their mother. My mothers are holding their children as best they can, enclosed as an image on the laptop monitor. It is a mother and child portrait, shaped by the economic realities of the gap between East and West.

Mom Egg Review

Current Issue
Mom Egg Review Vol. 12   2014 Paper, 150 pp. $18.00

Back Issues Available
The Mom Egg   Vol. 4   2006 Paper, 99 pp. $14.95
The Mom Egg   Vol. 5   2007 Paper, 101 pp. $14.95
The Mom Egg   Vol. 6   2008 Paper, 114 pp. $18.95
The Mom Egg   Vol. 7   2009 Paper, 124 pp. $18.00
The Mom Egg   Vol. 8 "Lessons"   2010 Paper, 120 pp. $18.00
The Mom Egg   Vol. 9   2011 Paper, 120 pp. $18.00
The Mom Egg   Vol. 10 "The Body"   2012 Paper, 120 pp. $18.00
The Mom Egg   Vol. 11 "Mother Tongue" 2013 Paper, 125 pp. $18.00

*Plus US shipping $2.50 for the first book, $1.00 for each additional book.
Email info@themomegg.com for info about discounts for quantity purchases and for classroom use, or for out-of-country shipping.

Subscribe to MER

Shipping is free for subscription copies!
Subscriptions start in 2015.

One year $16
Two years $29

Mail your order with a check to

Mom Egg Review
Half-Shell Press
PO Box 9037
Bardonia, NY 10954

contact: info@themomegg.com

or order on the web at
www.momeggreview.com (Click "Shop")

MOM EGG REVIEW

Made in the USA
Charleston, SC
06 March 2014